Dedication ...

Dedicated to my loved ones - My Husband, S. Shankar and our lovely offspring's - Ashwin and Aishwarya, for their sustained support in this writing. The inspiration as always, comes from the 'invisible hand' of encouragement from my parents and parents-in-law.

Preface ...

This book on Business Economics (Micro) is a culmination of several years of teaching and learning. It is a small venture towards kindling the students' interest in the rudimentaries of micro economics. The fundamental principles of economics have great applications in day to day life. An effort has been made to link economic theories with practical applications. The language is crisp and lucid. An attempt has been made to enhance clarity though appropriate tables, graphs (diagrams).

I sincerely thank Shri. Dineshbhai Furia and Shri Jignesh Furia, the publishers, for the confidence reposed in me and giving me this opportunity to reach out to the students of commerce and management.

I am grateful to the Dean, Faculty of Commerce, SPPU - Dr. Parag Kalkar and Associate Dean, Faculty of Commerce SPPU - Dr. Y. Mithare and the Chairman of the Board of Studies (Business Economics) Dr. S. Dhage and my colleagues for their valuable suggestions.

Nirali Prakahsan with its energetic and enthusiastic team comprising of Mr. Amol Mahabal, Akbar Shaikh, Prasad Chintakindi, Anjali Mule and Sachin Shinde have lent finishing touches to the book.

I humbly acknowledge the contribution of all those authors, writers and economists whose readings have played a significant role in the writing of this book.

Suggestions and feedback from readers are most welcome at niralipune@pragationline.com.

Dr. Girija Shankar

December 2019

■■■

Preface

Syllabus ...

1. Cost and Revenue

1.1 Concepts and Types of Cost – Economic Cost and Accounting Cost, Private Cost and Social Cost, Actual Cost and Opportunity Cost, Explicit Cost and Implicit Cost

1.2 Relation between Total Cost, Average Cost and Marginal Cost

1.3 Cost Curves in Short run and Long run

1.4 Concept of Total Revenue, Average Revenue and Marginal Revenue

2. Pricing Under Perfect Market Conditions

2.1 Pure Competition: Meaning and Features

2.2 Features of Perfect Competition

2.3 Price Determination in Perfect Competition

2.4 Equilibrium of Firm and Industry in Short Run and Long Run

3. Pricing Under Imperfect Market Conditions

3.1 Meaning of Imperfect Competition

3.2 Monopoly: Features and Equilibrium, Price Discrimination

3.3 Monopolistic Competition: Features and Equilibrium

3.4 Oligopoly: Concept and Features

3.5 Duopoly: Concept and Features

3.6 Comparison of Perfect and Imperfect Competition

4. Factor Pricing

4.1 Marginal Productivity Theory of Distribution

4.2 Rent: Meaning, Ricardian Theory of Rent, Modern Theory of Rent, Concept of Quasi Rent

4.3 Wages:

4.3.1 Meaning and Types of Wages:

(a) Minimum Wages, (b) Money Wages, (c) Real Wages, (d) Subsistence Wages, (e) Fair Wages

4.3.2 Backward Bending Supply Curve of Labour

4.3.3 Role of Collective Bargaining in Wage Determination

4.4 Interest: Meaning, Lonable Fund Theory, Liquidity Preference Theory

4.5 Profit: Meaning, Risk and Uncertainty Theory of Profit, Dynamic Theory of Profit, Innovation Theory of Profit

■■■

Contents ...

■■■

Unit **1...**

Cost and Revenue

Contents ...

Learning Objectives ...

- To understand the relation between Total Cost (TC), Average Cost (AC) and Marginal Cost (MC).
- To study the behaviour of Cost Curves in the Short-run and Long-run
- To learn the Concepts of Total Revenue (TR), Average Revenue (AR) and Marginal Revenue (MR)

1.1 CONCEPT AND TYPES OF COST

During the process of production, a number of factors (both fixed and variable) join hands. These factors are available only at a price. Expenses incurred on the factors of production are known as the cost of *production,* or in short, the *cost.* On the other hand, producer receives payments from the sale of goods produced. Such sale proceeds are referred to as *revenue* in economics.

The **accumulation, examination,** and **manipulation** of **cost data** for comparisons and **projections** is known as cost analysis.

The aim of the producer is to maximize his profits. Since profit is the difference between revenue and cost, profit maximization amounts to maximization of difference between revenue and cost, by increasing revenue and lowering cost. While the level of revenue is primarily determined by the market factors, the cost can be brought down either by producing the optimum level of output using the least cost combination of inputs or by increasing factor productivities or by improving the organisational efficiency. A profit maximizing firm needs to monitor revenue and cost continuously. Thus, the concepts of cost and revenue are very important in price theory. They exhibit not only the profits or losses earned by the firm, but also help in price and output determination. A rational producer chooses the production decision through the cost and revenue analysis.

Cost of production provides the floor to pricing. It helps managers to take correct decisions, like which price to quote, whether to place a particular order for inputs or not, whether to abandon or add a product to the existing product line, whether to expand or contract production, whether or not to use idle capacity, whether to buy or manufacture a product etc.

Production function as such does not reveal anything about the economic aspect of costs and prices. Once prices of factor inputs are known, the technological relationships implied by the production function can be used to derive the cost functions. Hence the theory of costs is a restatement of the theory of production in monetary terms.

Here we consider the costs of production of the firm. Firms must pay careful attention to costs because every unit of increase in cost reduces the firm's profits. But costs are important in economics for a deeper reason: firms will decide how much of a good to produce and sell depending on the price and the cost of the goods. More precisely, supply depends upon incremental or marginal cost. And the dependence of supply decisions on cost is true not only for perfect competitors but also for firms in the vast terrain of imperfect competition. Whatever the market structure, whether perfectly or imperfectly competitive, marginal cost is a key concept for understanding a firm's behaviour. It is necessary to understand different cost concept and their relevance or irrelevance in the decision making.

1.1.1 Types of Costs

Cost Classification on the Basis of Economic Concept

Demand estimation and forecasting demand in the future are, no doubt, two main problems in decision making by the executives of business firms. But there is another area- more complex and complicated, which is of great concern to managerial economics, viz., the cost of production. Profit is the difference between the total cost and the total revenue. Total revenue can be estimated by multiplying the total quantity of the output sold by its price (total output x price).It is not so simple with costs.

Some costs vary with output, some are fixed, yet some are hidden. Some costs are not recorded in the books of accounts, yet they are to be taken into account- these are opportunity costs, also called implicit costs. Making of effective and right decisions depends much on the proper calculation of the costs. If different types of costs are not properly understood, the managerial decisions are bound to be wrong and misleading.

1. Historical cost or Sunk cost and Replacement costs: Historical costs are the costs of an asset purchased in the past at the then prevailing price. They are regarded as **sunk cost**, as they cannot be retrieved from the business without loss. Sunk cost is an economic term for a sum paid in the past, which should no longer be relevant, hence these costs are irrelevant in decision making with the perspective of time. The cost of assets is shown at their historical cost in the conventional financial accounts. When the old asset wears out, it has to be replaced by a new one. However, replacement of an asset has to be done at the current price, which may be different from the price at which the asset was originally purchased in the past. Therefore, **replacement cost is defined as the cost to be incurred for replacing the same asset, at current prices.** If the prices remain stable over a considerable length of time, the historical and replacement cost will be on par with each other. But as we know, the prices of goods keep on increasing. Hence, the replacement cost may be much more than the historical cost of the book value of the asset. Suppose the book cost of the machine is ₹ 1000 the price at which the machine was purchased in the past, say 3 years ago. This is its historical cost. However, if the current market price of the machine is ₹ 1100 and if the machine is to be replaced by a new one, the firm has to pay ₹ 1100. Hence the replacement cost of the machine is ₹ 1100. *While projecting future costs, it is necessary to take into account, the replacement cost of the asset rather than the historical cost.*

Historical cost of a plant or machine is used for accounting purpose, and replacement cost at the current price plays a vital role in business decisions regarding future projects.

2. Private Cost and Social Cost:

Private Cost: It is a producer's or supplier's cost of providing goods or services. It includes internal costs incurred for inputs, labour, rent and depreciation but excludes external costs incurred as environmental damage. Private cost is the cost borne by an individual or firm directly involved in a transaction.

Social Cost: Social costs of a firm are those that the society in general has to bear because of the firm's activities. Pollution caused by industrial waste and emission is a typical example of social cost. Social cost has 2 components:

(a) Private cost of the firm.

(b) Social costs paid by the society.

The increasing awareness of social cost in the corporate section has given rise to the concept of Corporate Social Responsibility (CSR). Parks maintained by industries, community projects and relief works undertaken by corporates during natural disasters such as earthquakes and floods are classic examples of CSR exhibited by Corporate houses.

3. Direct Cost and Indirect Cost: There are some costs which can be directly attributed to the production of a unit of a given product, e.g. cost of labour, raw materials and machine hours required to produce a unit output. Such costs are *direct costs* and can easily be separated, ascertained and be imputed to a unit of output. This is because these costs vary with the output units. However there are other costs which cannot be separated and clearly attributed to individual units of production, eg expenses on account of fuel and power, office and administrative expenses and depreciation of plant and equipment. These costs are therefore classified as 'Indirect' or 'Overhead' costs in the accounting process. **If the cost is separable per unit of output, it is a direct cost for the accountant, and if it cannot be separated per unit of output, then it is an indirect overhead cost.**

4. Real Cost and Actual Cost:

Real Cost: Real Costs are more or less social and psychological in nature and non-quantifiable in money terms. Since real costs do not cause any outflow of cash or any increase in liabilities, accountants do not consider these costs as such. But decision makers cannot ignore them. The modern concept of compensation packages is strongly driven by the real cost component of total cost, as besides nominal salary, employers try to compensate for leisure, social and family needs.

Actual Cost: It is an actual amount paid or incurred, as opposed to estimated cost or standard cost. In contracting, actual costs amount includes direct labour, direct material and other direct charges.

5. Opportunity Cost or Alternative Cost: There is no difficulty in recording the cost of inputs actually purchased at the market prices, such as the cost of labour, cost of raw materials, fuel, power, etc. But the problem arises in imputing cost to self-owned inputs, such as the services of owner manager, the self –owned funds invested in the business and the self-owned premises in which the firm is located. These implicit costs are calculated on the basis of their opportunity cost. **Opportunity cost refers to what an input could earn in its next best alternative job.** E.g. when the owner chooses to work as the manager of his own firm, then he has to forgo the next best alternative viz. to work as a manager in somebody else's firm. While imputing salary for his services as owner manager we must consider the opportunity cost by him of earning an annual income of ₹ 30000 as a manager elsewhere. Hence the opportunity cost as the owner manager of his own firm will be equal to ₹ 30000 which he could have earned in the next best alternative job. While imputing opportunity cost, care must be taken to consider earnings not in any alternative job but the next best alternative job under the same conditions. The calculation of opportunity costs of all factors in the production process is immensely important for sound decision making. *It ensures that all resources are employed in their most efficient uses.*

6. Incremental and Marginal cost: Incremental costs are defined as the change in the overall costs that result in a particular decision being made. Incremental costs may include both fixed and variable costs. In the short period incremental costs will consist of variable costs –costs of additional labour, additional power, raw materials, fuel etc., which is the result of a new decision being taken by the firm. A new decision may involve the purchase of additional capital assets and hence incremental costs may consist of fixed costs also.

Incremental costs may also be the result of increase in the output level, or it may simply be due to the use of new techniques to produce the same level of output. Generally, of course incremental costs are the result of a decision to expand the output with the help of the existing plant and equipment or to expand the capacity of the firm by installing more machines or big machines.

Marginal costs are the change in the total cost for a one unit changes in the output level. In other words, marginal costs are the cost of producing an additional or extra unit of output. Suppose the cost of producing 100 units of the output is ₹ 1000 and the cost of producing 101 units of the output in ₹ 1011. Then the marginal cost is ₹ 11. Now we see this example, the total cost of producing 100 units is ₹ 1000 and the firm decides to produce extra 50 units, which takes the total cost of 150 units to ₹ 1600. The incremental cost is ₹ 600 and the marginal cost is (600/50) ₹ 12. It is, of course, assumed that the firm can expand its output in bulk quantity by 50 units at a time. Thus, incremental costs are the aggregate change in the costs (ΔC) as a result of a decision of the firm. Incremental costs help in estimating marginal cost. Marginal cost is found out by a ratio between change in total cost due to one unit change in output and unit change in input. $\frac{\Delta C}{\Delta X}$

where ΔC is increase in total cost due to a unit change in output and

ΔX is a unit change in output.

In calculating incremental costs, a precaution must be taken to include only those costs that change as a result of the decision. Sunk costs or the costs which are already incurred and which do not change as a result of the decision should not be included as *Allocated Overheads*. Thus the cost of plant already erected, machines, and equipment already installed and lying idle, having no positive opportunity costs, must not be included, while taking new decision in calculating incremental costs. Otherwise the decision would be wrong or inferior.

The decision maker must ensure that incremental costs are calculated on the basis of relevant costs only; and all irrelevant costs- sunk costs, historical costs, cost of fixed factors having no positive opportunity costs- are to be excluded. This is very important. The main objective of the incremental cost is to enable a firm to find out whether a proposed decision will be profitable or not. For this purpose the firm should calculate incremental revenue (change in total revenue) resulting from the new decision, and then compare it with the new decision to find out whether the new decision will be profitable or not. Obviously, if aggregate incremental revenue is greater than incremental costs, the profits of the firm will increase (or loss if any will decrease). Incremental costs are important particularly in taking output decisions in the short period.

7. Accounting Concept of Cost and Economic Concept of Cost: Explicit costs are the costs incurred by the firm. These costs refer to the money payments made for the use of raw materials, payments to the labour employed, money costs of power, fuel , rental for the use of the land, interest on loans taken etc. These are the payments made for the contractual obligations and are recorded in the books of account. Accountants traditionally include only actual expenditure in costs i.e. for tax purposes the **accountant's definition of costs includes only explicit cost.**

Implicit Costs

However in economic sense, there are other costs which must be taken into account while calculating profits. There are other services for which no contractual payments are made i.e. no actual expenditure is incurred. These are the costs of the self employed and the self owned resources of the firm. These costs are called *Implicit Costs.* The examples of such costs are:opportunity cost of the owner's services ,say, as the manager of the firm, opportunity cost of the land belonging to the owner of the firm, and normal return equal to the market rate of the interest on the owner's own capital invested in the business. These implicit costs are not included by the accountant of the firm in its accounting statements. However these costs are considered relevant by the economists while calculating the economic profits of the firm. There is only one implicit cost that appears in the profit and loss account, and that is depreciation charges which appear in the accounting process in addition to the explicit costs. However other implicit costs (wages for the owner's own service as manager, rent for self-owned land, interest on the owners own funds invested in the business) are not included in the accounting process. It is necessary to include both explicit and implicit costs to arrive at the economic profits.

8. Opportunity Cost, Economic Cost and Accounting Cost: In economics, costs include explicit and implicit costs.

Explicit Costs are the actual out of pocket expenditures of the firm to purchase or hire the inputs it requires in production. These expenditures include the wages to hire labour, interest on borrowed capital, rent on land and buildings and the expenditures on raw materials. Accountants traditionally include only actual expenditures in costs i.e. for tax purposes the *accountant's definition of cost includes only explicit cost.*

Implicit costs refer to the value of the inputs owned and used by the firm in its own production processes. The value of these owned inputs must be imputed or estimated from what these inputs could earn in their best alternative use. Implicit costs include the maximum wages that the entrepreneur could earn in working for someone else in a similar capacity (say, as the manager of another firm), and the highest return that the firm could obtain from investing in capital elsewhere and renting out its land and other inputs to others. The inputs owned and used by the firm in its own production process are not free to the firm, even though the firm can use them without any actual or explicit expenditures. Economists always include both explicit and *implicit costs,* and *opportunity costs.*

Opportunity cost

Opportunity cost is the cost which is not actually incurred, but would have been incurred in the absence of employment of self-owned factors. The concept of opportunity cost was popularized by American writers. It occupies a very important place in modern economic analysis. *Opportunity cost of any input is the next best alternative use that is sacrificed by its present use.* It is measured by the value of factors of production used in producing a good, when put to the next best alternative use. In other words, it indicates what a factor could earn in the next best use. Opportunity cost reflects the benefits we give up to select the most preferred choice. For example, if a farmer decides to grow wheat instead of rice, the opportunity cost of the wheat would be the rice, which he might have grown rather. Thus, opportunity cost is the cost of foregone alternative. If we produce more of one thing, resources have to be withdrawn from other uses, as these are scarce. In the words of *Lipsey,* " The opportunity cost of using any factor is what is currently foregone by using it." Opportunity cost is also the opportunity lost or sacrificed. To quote Watson "Cost of anything is the value of the alternative or the opportunity that is sacrificed".

Implicit cost incurred by the firm is actually the opportunity cost of the factor owned by him. By employing this factor in the firm, the producer loses the opportunity of earning the factor income, had it been employed elsewhere. Thus, the opportunity cost of a factor input is nothing but a potential return from the next best alternative use of that factor.

Opportunity cost is also the minimum price necessary to retain a factor in the current employment. Joan Robinson calls it *transfer earning.* Since a firm has to pay to owners of factors what they can secure in alternative employment, opportunity cost is also known as *alternative cost.*

Opportunity cost of a good is not simply any other alternative good that could be produced with the same factors. It is only the most valuable (or next best alternative) good, which the same factors or nearly the same value of factors could produce.

Significance of the concept of Opportunity Cost

1. The concept of opportunity cost is highly useful to each and every economic unit. Each cost concept can be expressed in terms of opportunity cost. Every action that we take involves an opportunity cost, as cost of getting something involves losing something else.

For example:

(a) For a student, the cost of seeing a movie may be the book, whose purchase he has foregone.

(b) For the consumer, the opportunity cost of buying a commodity is the price; he pays for it in monetary terms.

(c) For the government, the cost of building a college may be the hospital sacrificed.

(d) For the society, the cost of setting up an ammunition factory may be the bread and butter sacrificed.

2. Opportunity cost has wide economic implications. It is important in the context of factors of production. As supply of the factors is limited, a factor can be utilized in one use (or at present) by sacrificing its use for other purpose (in future). It helps us to know, how limited resources get allocated in different branches of production.
3. It can be used to determine the factor price. The concept is especially relevant for an industry which must pay wages which are at least equal to what are being paid in other industries. Otherwise, labour will shift to another industry. Thus the opportunity cost concept is useful in short term decisions like sales strategy, inventory management, hiring and firing of labour.
4. It is also applicable in investment planning to make a choice of best alternative after evaluating all available alternatives carefully. A profit oriented firm must consider opportunity cost besides explicit cost in order to use all the resources most economically.

Limitations of the concept of Opportunity Cost

1. It is only applicable to those factors which have alternative uses. Thus, if no sacrifice is involved, then the opportunity cost is zero. Even though the *actual cost* or the *acquisition cost* or the *historical cost* (the cost at which the factor was originally acquired or purchased) was substantial.
2. Further, foregone alternatives are often not clearly ascertainable due to imperfect knowledge of factor owners and imperfections in the market.

1.2 BEHAVIOUR OF COST CURVES

A firm's cost functions will vary, depending on whether they are based on the **short run period** or **long run period.** Here 'period' or 'time' refers to the functional or operational time period. Short run and long run do not refer to any calendar time. They are sets of conditions and not periods of time. A short run period is one during which certain factors like factory buildings, number of machines, land, managerial staff etc remain fixed. Hence these factors are called **fixed factors.** So, in a short run period, the size of the plant of a firm and its scale of production would remain constant. However in the short run, the other factors such as labour, raw materials and power can be varied in amount. Hence these factors are called **variable factors.**

A **long run period** is one during which all the factors of production can be fully varied in amount by a firm i.e. in the long run, all the factors become variable. So, in the long run, the size of the plant of a firm and its scale of production can be fully increased or decreased.

1.3 (A) SHORT RUN COSTS

1. **Total Fixed Cost (TFC)**

   Fixed costs are those which are independent of output i.e. they do not change with changes in output. These costs are a 'fixed' amount which must be incurred by a firm in the short run, whether the output is small or large. Even if the firm closes down for some time in the short run but remains in business, these costs have to be borne by it. **Fixed costs are also known as sunk costs or indirect costs by economists and overhead costs or supplementary cost by business people**. These include charges such as contractual rent, insurance fee, maintenance costs, property taxes, interest on capital invested, minimum administrative expenses such as manager's salary, watchman's wages etc. Thus fixed costs are those which are incurred in hiring the fixed factors of production whose amounts cannot be altered in the short run.

2. **Total Variable Cost (TVC)**

   Variable costs on the other hand are those costs which are incurred on the employment of variable factors of production whose amount can be altered in the short run. Thus the TVCs change with changes in output in the short run i.e. they increase or decrease when the output rises or falls. These costs include payment such as wages of labour employed, prices of the raw materials, fuel and power used the expenses on transport etc. If a firm shuts down production for some time in the short run, then it will not use the variable factors of production and will not therefore incur any variable costs. Variable costs are made only when some amount of output is produced and the TVCs increase with the increase in the level of production. Variable costs are also called **prime costs** or direct costs.

3. Total Cost

Total cost of a business is the sum of its total fixed costs and total variable costs.

TC = TFC + TVC

TC increases as level of output increases.

Cost - output relationship in the short run:

Consider the following table:

Table 1.1

Total Output (Q)	Total Fixed Cost (TFC)	Total Variable cost (TVC)	Total Cost (TC)	Average Fixed Cost (AFC)	Average Variable cost (AVC)	Average Total cost or Average Cost (AC)	Marginal Cost (MC)
0	300	0	300	–	–	–	–
1	300	60	360	300	60	360	60
2	300	110	410	150	55	205	50
3	300	160	460	100	53	153	50
4	300	200	500	75	50	125	40
5	300	260	560	60	52	112	60
6	300	360	660	50	60	110	100
7	300	510	810	43	73	116	150
8	300	710	1,010	38	89	126	200
9	300	1,060	1,360	33	118	151	350

Behaviour of TC, TFC and TVC

Considering the above table: 1.1 it can be seen that:

1. TFC remains constant at all levels of output i.e. FCs are independent of output.
2. TVC varies directly with level of output. When output is zero, TVC is also zero. Upto output level 4, TVC **increases** at a **decreasing rate,** beyond that output rate, TVC **increases** at an **increasing rate.** This characteristic of TVC function results from the operation of the law of diminishing marginal returns. At small output rates, increases in the utilisation of variable inputs may bring about increases in their productivity, causing TVC to increase with output, but at a decreasing rate. Beyond a point, however, there are diminishing marginal returns from the variable input, with the result that TVCs increase at an increasing rate.
3. TC = TFC + TVC. Change in TCs is entirely due to change in TVC, since there are no changes in TFC.

All this can be diagrammatically represented as follows:

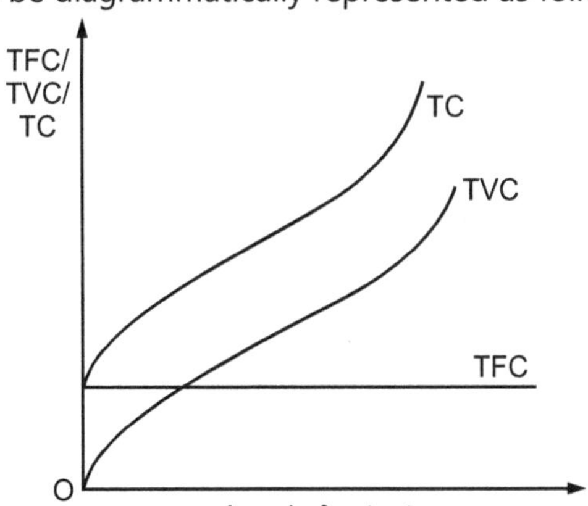

Fig. 1.1: TC, TFC and TVC

TC, TFC and TVC

In the above Fig. 1.1, it can be seen that:

1. TFC is a straight horizontal line parallel to the X axis.
2. TVC begins from origin, initially rises gradually but eventually becomes steeper because TVC rises rapidly as output increases.

3. TC is derived by the vertical addition of TFC and TVC. It takes the same shape as TVC. When TVC changes its rate of change, TC also changes in the same manner.

4. Average Fixed Cost (AFC)

AFC means fixed cost per unit of output. Hence,

$$AFC = \frac{TFC}{Q} \text{ i.e. } \frac{\text{Total fixed cost}}{\text{Total units of output}}$$

Since TFC is constant, AFC will steadily fall as output increases. Therefore AFC curve slopes downward throughout its length. As output increases, TFC spreads over more and more units and therefore AFC becomes less and less and when Q becomes very large, AFC approaches zero (but not equal to zero). AFC has the shape of a rectangular hyperbola. Refer Fig. 1.2.

5. Average Variable Cost (AVC)

AVC means variable cost per unit of output. Hence

$$AVC = \frac{TVC}{Q} \text{ i.e. } \frac{\text{Total variable cost}}{\text{Total units of output}}$$

Initially AVC will decline due to increasing returns, reaches a minimum (Point C) and later will rise steeply due to the law of diminishing returns. Therefore AVC is U shaped. Refer Fig. 1.2.

6. Average Total Cost (ATC) or Average Cost (AC)

This is total cost per unit of output. Hence

$$ATC = \frac{TC}{Q} = \frac{TFC + TVC}{Q} = \frac{TFC}{Q} + \frac{TVC}{Q} = AFC + AVC$$

The ATC is also U shaped. This is because of the fact that ATC is the sum of AFC and AVC. As output increases, both AFC and AVC decrease, hence ATC must also decrease. But beyond some point, ATC must increase because increases in AVC eventually more than offset decreases in AFC. However ATC achieves its minimum (point B) after AVC, because the increases in AVC are for a time more than offset by decreases in AFC. Refer Fig. 1.2.

Reason for U-shape of the short run average cost curve (SAC): The AC curve in the short run (**SAC**) has a pronounced U shape. In the short run, the plant of the firm is fixed while other inputs are variable. Production is subject to the **law of variable proportions.** As output is increased to approach the capacity or short-period optimum output of the plant, overhead costs per unit continue to fall. Till output reaches the capacity of the plant, other inputs are lower in proportion than what the 'optimum' proportions are in relation to the fixed plant; average cost will continue to fall. After the capacity output is reached, average cost begins to rise because the variable inputs become 'too much' for the plant of fixed size. Thus, the 'U' shape of the short run average cost curve is due to the non-proportional returns at a *given scale of output*. The non-proportional returns can, in turn, be explained by *the technical reasons* that underlie increasing returns to the variable inputs (factors) at first and then diminishing returns to them, once the 'capacity' output of the plant is exceeded.

7. Marginal Cost (MC):

MC is the addition to TC caused by producing one more unit of output. Hence

$$MC = \frac{\Delta TC}{\Delta Q} \quad \text{where} \quad \Delta TC = \text{change in TC}$$

$$\Delta Q = \text{Change in output}$$

OR

$$MC_n = TC_n - TC_{n-1}$$

Since $TC = TFC + TVC$

So, $MC_n = (TFC_n + TVC_n) - (TFC_{n-1} + TVC_{n-1})$

$$= TFC_n + TVC_n - TFC_{n-1} - TVC_n - 1$$

(Since $TFC_n = TFC_{n-1} = TFC$)

$$= TVC_n - TVC_{n-1}$$

MC is independent of TFC

MC falls initially, reaches a minimum and then rises. In other words, beyond some point it becomes more and more costly for the firm to produce yet another unit of output. MC is U shaped (or shape of a hockey stick or umbrella handle.)

MC reaches a minimum (point A) at a much earlier level of Q,(output) starts rising and on its upward path, passes, through the minimum of AVC (point C) and minimum of ATC (or AC) (point B). Refer Fig. 1.2.

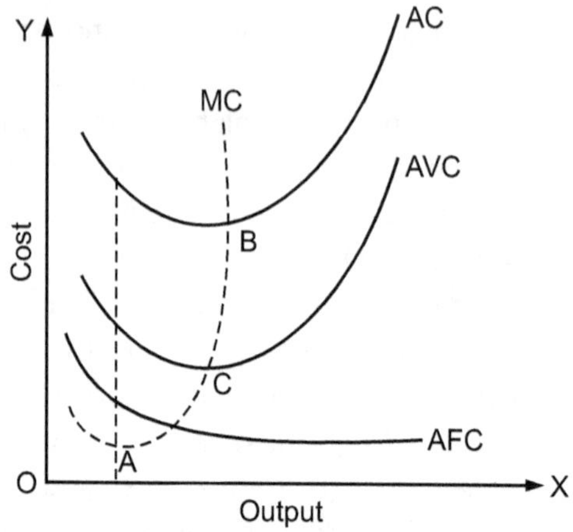

Fig. 1.2: Relationship among AVC, AC and MC Curves

Relationship between Average Cost (AC) and Marginal Cost (MC)

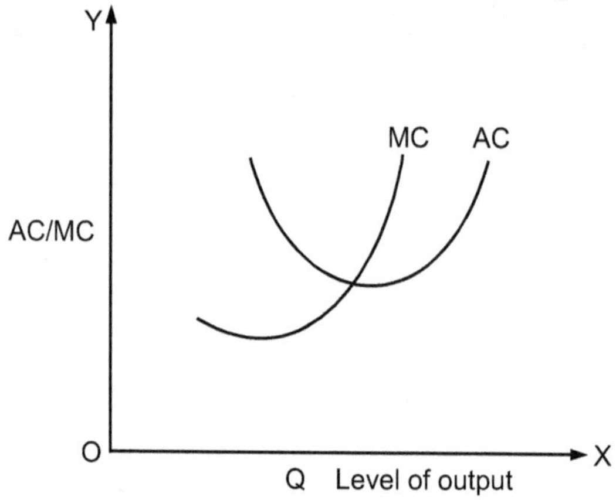

Fig. 1.3: AC and MC Curves

AC and MC

Both MC and AC are derived from TC. The relationship between AC and MC must be noted. In the above Fig. 1.3, it can be seen that:

(a) When **AC falls** with an increase in output, **MC is lower than AC.** i.e. MC curve lies below the AC curve. However, it is not necessary that MC should fall throughout this stage. Actually MC rises earlier than AC.

(b) At the level of optimum output, AC **is minimum and constant. Here AC = MC.**

(c) When **AC rises** with increase in output, **MC is higher than AC** i.e. MC curve lies above the AC curve.

In brief, it can be said that MC intersects AC at its minimum point. Both are U-shaped curves on account of the operation of the law of variable proportions.

Referring to Fig. 1.2, it can be seen that, as long as AC curve is falling, MC is less than AC, i.e. MC pulls AC downwards. However, MC falls more rapidly and reaches its minimum point 'A' earlier than AC reaches its own minimum point 'B'. Therefore, MC starts rising from point 'A' to point 'B'. AC is still falling upto point 'B'. Further, beyond point 'B', both MC and AC rise, but, MC rises more sharply. When MC rises above AC, it pulls AC upwards. Similar relationship holds between MC and AVC too. MC intersects both AVC and AC (from below) at their respective minimum points in that order.

The relationship between AC and MC is more easily understood if explained in terms of cricket batting averages. Let us assume that a cricketer's batting average is 60 runs. If in his next innings he scores less than 60, say 52, his average will fall because his marginal score is less than his average score. However in the next innings (average being 60 runs) if he scores more than 60, say 64, his average will rise because now his marginal score is more than his average score (60 runs.) Similarly if he now plays an innings (with average being 60 runs) in which he scores just 60, then his average and marginal scores will be equal. His average score will neither rise nor fall.

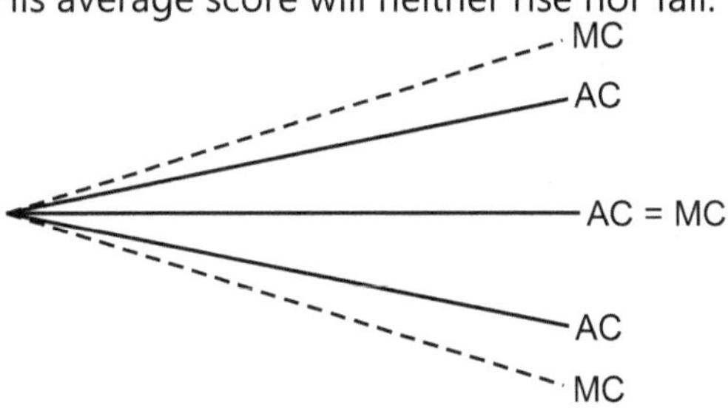

Fig. 1.4

In Fig. 1.4 it is seen that:

(a) When the slope of AC curve is negative (i.e. AC curve is falling), MC will be less than AC and thus lie below AC.

(b) When the slope of AC is positive (i.e. AC is rising). MC will be greater than AC and lie above it.

(c) When the slope of AC is equal to zero (i.e. AC is minimum), MC is equal to AC.

On the other hand, if as in Fig. 1.5 the average curve (the average product curve - AP) were shaped like an inverted U the corresponding marginal curve (the marginal product curve– MP) would always cut the AP curve at its highest point (point C).

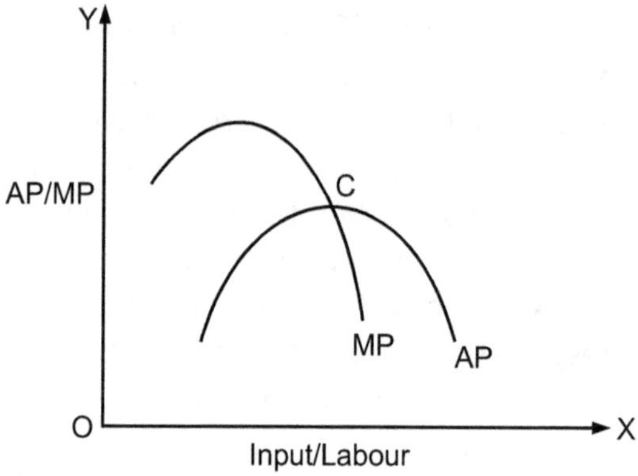

Fig. 1.5: AP and MP Curves

1.3 (B) LONG RUN COST

The long run is a period during which the firm can vary all its inputs. There are no fixed factors. Therefore, there is no FCs. All costs are VCs. In the long period, the firm can alter the size of plant and change the scale of production in order to expand or contract output according to demand by having more or less of the various factors of production. The long run consists of all possible short run situations among which the entrepreneur can choose. In the words of Leftwich, "The long run is a series of alternative short run situations into any one of which the firm can move. The long run may be compared with the action sequence of a motion picture. If we stop the film and look at a single picture we have a short run concept."

In the short run, plant size is fixed (by plant size we mean capital equipment, machinery, land etc.) The plant size cannot be increased or reduced. Therefore a firm is tied with a given plant.

But in the long run, a firm moves from one plant to another, a firm can go in for larger plant if it has to increase its output and a smaller plant if it has to reduce its output.

Long Run Total Cost Curves

Long run costs are called as *planning costs or ex-ante costs,* as the firm has to plan its future course of action from a wide range of options. It may expand the existing plant, install a new plant, change the management style, etc. Long run total cost (LTC) curves showing the relationship between output and total cost are derived from the long-run production functions in which all inputs are variable. LTC curve can be derived from short-run total cost (STC) curves.

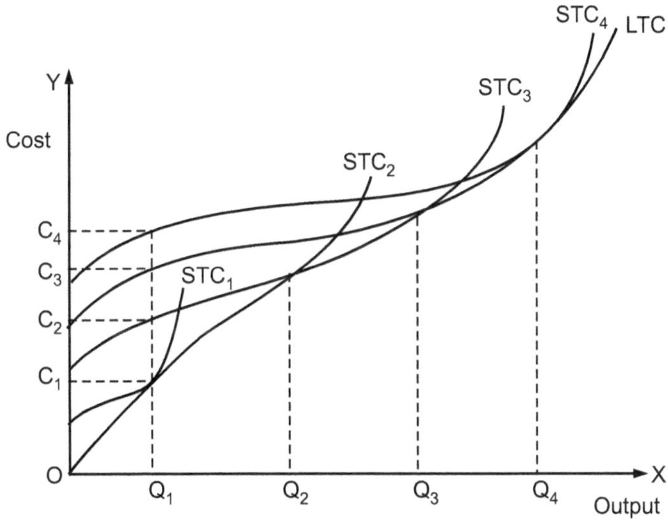

Fig. 1.6: Derivation of Long-run Total Cost Curve from Short-run Total Cost Curves

The above figure depicts the derivation of LTC curve from STC curves. There is a family of short run cost curves, one for each capacity, depending on the output it wants to produce in the long-run. The long-run envelops on the short run cost curves, for the long run cost cannot exceed the short run cost. The long run and the short run costs are equal only at output levels Q_1, Q_2, Q_3, and Q_4 which correspond to the point of tangency between LAC and SAC curves. It is also clear from the figure that when output is small, the total cost is less for a small plant than for a large plant. Likewise, for larger outputs, larger plants are more suitable. Such plants remain underutilised for small output, while a small plant is inadequate for large outputs. For output OQ_1, the smallest plant is most appropriate, as total cost OC_1 under this plant is less than that for any other plant size (OC_2, OC_3 and OC_4). It is not viable to produce OQ_2 or more output with such a small plant. For output levels of OQ_2, OQ_3 and OQ_4, plants with short run cost curves STC_2, STC_3 and STC_4, respectively are most suitable.

Like short run variable cost curve, the LTC curve first increases at a decreasing rate, then at an increasing rate. (Refer Fig. 1.6). This curve starts from the origin implying thereby that in the long run, if nothing is produced, no resources will be used. While the shape of short run variable cost curve is due to the law of variable proportions in the short-run, the shape of the LTC curve is due to the existence of returns to scale. Similar to short run variable cost curve, the long run total cost curve is initially concave from below and thereafter it is convex from below.

Long Run Average Cost (LAC)

In the short run, there is only one short run average cost (SAC) curve corresponding to one (fixed) plant. However, in the long run, a firm has a number of alternatives with regard to the scale of production. For each scale of production, the firm has an appropriate short run average cost curve. The long run average cost (LAC) curve can be derived from a number of short run average cost curves, corresponding to different plant sizes. LAC depicts the least possible AC for producing all levels of output. The LAC curve is the envelope of the various SAC curves. It is drawn as a tangent to all the SAC_3. (Refer Fig. 1.7)

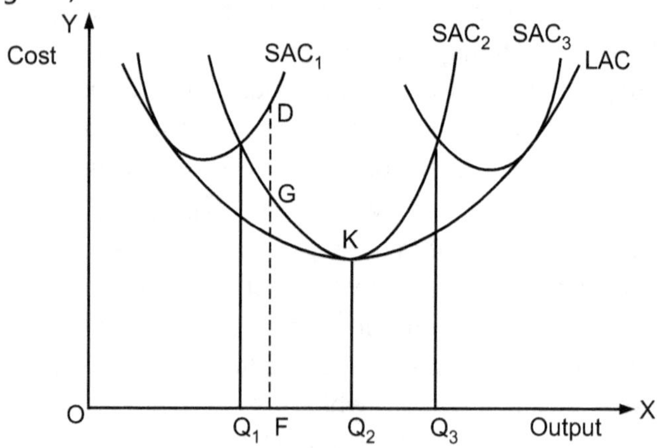

Fig. 1.7

In the above figure, SAC_1, SAC_2, and SAC_3 represent three successively increasing sizes of plant of the firm. Each plant is suitable for a particular range of output. Within this range, output can be varied by varying the quantity of variable inputs. If the firm starts production with small plant, (represented by SAC_1), it can operate this plant with the least possible cost for various levels of output up to OQ_1. For producing an output level beyond OQ_1, (on account of increase in demand), average cost in smaller plant is higher (DF>GF). Thus in the long run, the firm sets up a medium plant (bigger sized plant) represented by SAC_2. The average cost of this plant is lower than the small plant. For the medium sized plant (SAC_2) point K is the minimum point, corresponding to output level OQ_2 If the firm anticipates a rise in demand beyond OQ_3, it will install a large plant represented by SAC_3 to reduce the cost per unit. The LAC curve is a U shaped, continuous curve, but the U shape is less pronounced than the SAC curve.

The LAC curve can only be tangential to an SAC. It cannot cut any SAC curve. This is because for any given output, average cost cannot be higher in the long run than in the short run. The reason is that any adjustment which will reduce cost in the short run is also possible in the long run. On the other hand, it is always not possible in the short run to produce a given level of output in the cheapest possible way. It is impossible to change the amounts used of *all* factors of production in the short run. But they can all be altered in the long run. Hence it can be concluded that the LAC curve can never cut a SAC curve. It is only tangential to the SAC curves.

The LAC curve is called on **'envelope' curve** since it envelops or supports a family of SAC curves from below.

Only one SAC is tangential to LAC at its (SAC's) minimum–that SAC which is tangential to LAC at LAC's minimum.

SACs tangential to LAC (when LAC is falling) to the left of LAC's minimum and tangential to LAC at a point left of their minimum (when SAC is falling.)

SACs tangential to LAC (when LAC is rising) to the right of its minimum are tangential to LAC at a point on the right of their minimum (when SAC is increasing) (Refer Fig. 1.7)

Explanation of U shape of LAC curve

The U-shape of the LAC curve can be explained through the law of returns to scale. With increase in the scale of operation, LAC curve initially slopes downward due to the economies of scale (which explain increasing returns to scale). In this situation, the proportionate rise in long run cost is less than proportionate rise in the scale of operation. However, when diseconomies set in, the LAC curves turns upwards (which explain diminishing returns to scale) reflecting the increase in the long run average cost of production.

When a firm expands in the long run, it tends to reap the benefits of economies of large scale production (internal economies of scale). On account of these advantages, the firm's long run total cost increases slowly with output. As a result, long run average cost declines. These economies of scale can be distinguished into *real economies and pecuniary economies.*

Real economies are associated with a reduction in physical quantity of inputs, raw materials, various kinds of labour and capital required per unit of output, when the firm expands the scale of operations.

Pecuniary economies are realised from paying lower prices for the inputs used in the production and distribution of the product, as the size of the firm increases.

Once the economies of scale have been exploited and the LAC has reached its minimum point, further expansion in output leads to diseconomies of scale. The diseconomies are the disadvantages, which accrue to the firm on account of over expansion of the scale of operation beyond its optimal size. These diseconomies may be technical, managerial or of other types. (Refer 3.4)

Explanation of the position of the LAC curve

The internal economies and diseconomies determine the shape of the LAC curve. But the position of this curve depends on *external economies and diseconomies* .While the external economies cause a downward shift in the LAC curve, the external diseconomies result in an upward shift in the LAC curve.

Costs of a firm depend not only on its own output level, but also on the output level of the whole industry. This can be explained through external economies and diseconomies of scale, which accrue to the firms as a result of the expansion in the output of the whole industry. This can be illustrated through Fig. 1.8.

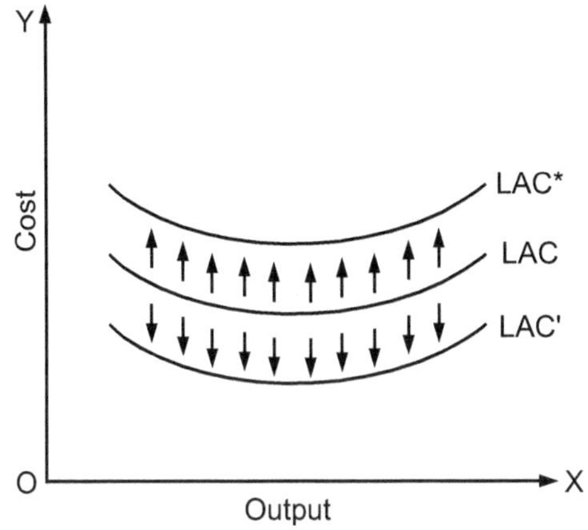

Fig. 1.8: Shift in LAC Curve (External Economies and Diseconomies)

In Fig. 1.8, external economies lower the long-run average cost at each level of output. Consequently, the LAC curve shifts downwards to LAC^1. Similarly, the LAC curve shifts upwards to LAC^* owing to external diseconomies. As a result, every level of output can only be produced with a higher cost per unit. Similar shifts are possible in LMC curve also on account of external economies (downward shift) and external diseconomies (upward shift).

Long run Marginal Cost Curve

The long run marginal cost (LMC) curve shows the minimum amount by which cost is increased each time, when output is increased or the maximum amount of total cost that can be reduced, when output is reduced. LMC curve is derived from the short run marginal cost (SMC) curves by considering the points of intersection of the SMCs, with vertical lines drawn from the points of tangency of corresponding SAC and LAC to the X-axis. This is illustrated in Fig. 1.9.

In the long run, if the firm wants to produce OQ_1 output, it will choose the plant corresponding to SAC_1. For this level of output, LAC curve is tangent to SAC_1 at point 'A'. The corresponding LMC will be equal to SMC_1 (i.e. BQ_1) at point 'B' corresponding to OQ_1level of output. This happens, because, when LAC is equal to SAC, LMC will also be equal to SMC. Thus, the LMC curve passes through point 'B'. Further, if OQ_2 output is produced, the firm will choose the plant corresponding to SAC_2. For this level of output, 'E' is the point on LAC curve, where both SAC_2 and SMC_2 are equal. The LMC curve will thus, pass through point 'E'. This implies that the production of output level of OQ_2 in the long run involves marginal cost of EQ_2. Finally, for output level of OQ_3, the LMC is equal to SMC_3 corresponding to the point of tangency between LAC and SAC_3 at point 'C'. The SMC_3 corresponding to this point (or OQ_3 level of output) is given by point 'D'. This is the point through which LMC curve will pass. LMC for output level OQ_3 is equal to DQ_3.

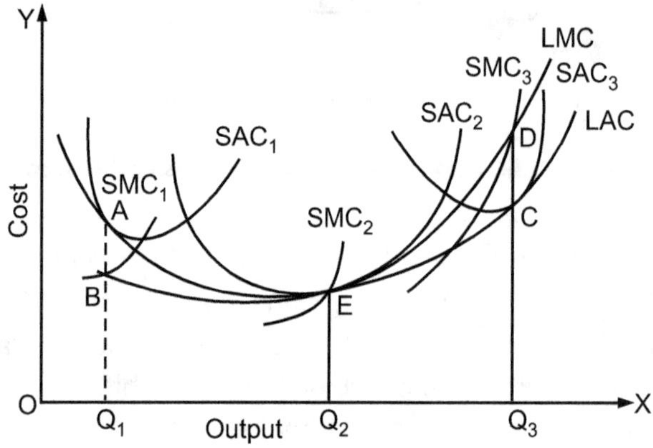

Fig. 1.9: Long Run Marginal Cost Curve

The LMC curve is derived by joining points 'B', 'E' and 'D'. This curve passes through those points of SMCs, which correspond to respective tangency points of short run average cost curves with LAC curve. *The LMC can thus be defined as the locus of those points on the SMC curves, which correspond to the optimum plant size (and not the optimum output, i,e, the point of minimum SACs) for each output.*

Relationship between LAC and LMC

The relationship between LAC and LMC (long run) is same as the one between AC and MC (short run). LMC curve cuts LAC curve at its minimum point as shown in Fig. 1.10.

From Fig. 1.10 it can be observed that:

1. When LAC is falling, LMC < LAC;
2. When LAC is rising, LMC> LAC and
3. When LAC is minimum, LMC = LAC.

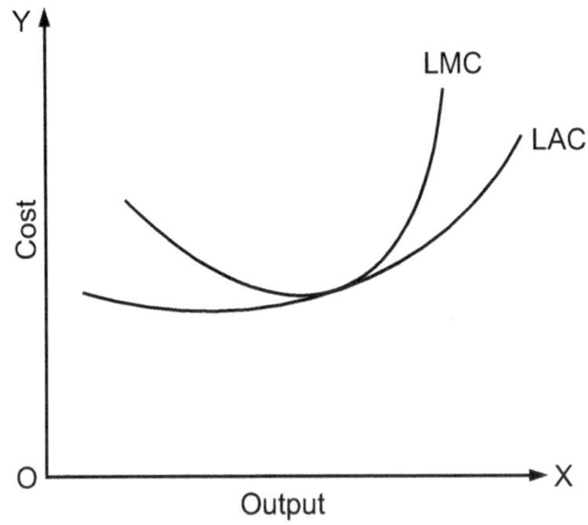

Fig. 1.10: Relationship between LAC and LMC

Modern Theory of Costs

The U-shaped cost curves (with only one level of optimal output) of the traditional theory have been questioned by several economists on theoretical as well as on empirical grounds. There are several factors which force a firm to have a *built-in reserve capacity,* thereby changing the shapes of cost curves.

(i) Firms which produce products having stable demand growth like steel, aluminium, cement etc. must provide for excess capacity. Otherwise, the firm will not be able to meet additional demand requirement at lower costs.

(ii) Reserve capacity gives greater flexibility for repairs of broken down machinery without disrupting the smooth flow of the production process.

(iii) Reserve capacity enables the firm to meet seasonal as well as cyclical fluctuation in demand with no additional holding costs,

(iv) Reserve capacity also allows the firm to make minor changes in the product to suit the changing tastes and requirements of the customers.

(v) Reserve capacity enables the firms to use better technology allowing them to produce more, whenever need arises.

(vi) The reserve capacity in land, building and scarce skilled human resources allows the firms to expand their operations smoothly.

Long run costs under Modern Theory of Costs

The shape of the LAC curve has attracted the attention of economists due to the serious policy implications of large scale production. Several arguments have been put forward to explain why the LAC curve is L-shaped rather than U-shaped. L-shape of LAC implies that it does not rise even at very large scale of output. According to modern economists, it was unrealistic to expect the emergence of diseconomies at least over the scales of production, which are generally operated in the real industrial world.

Modern theorists contend that the long-run average cost comprise of production and managerial cost. Production costs fall steeply to begin with and then gradually, as the scale of production increases. The reduction in production costs is the result of technical economies of large scale production, which are considerable in the initial phase of production. The problem of relatively decreased economies of scale at higher scales of operation can be overcome by the invention of new techniques. In the modern world of rapid technological change, this is not difficult. Thus the production costs fall smoothly at very large scales of production. This fall in technical costs, according to components of the modern approach, offsets the probable rise of managerial costs at very large scales of output. This is shown in Fig. 1.11.

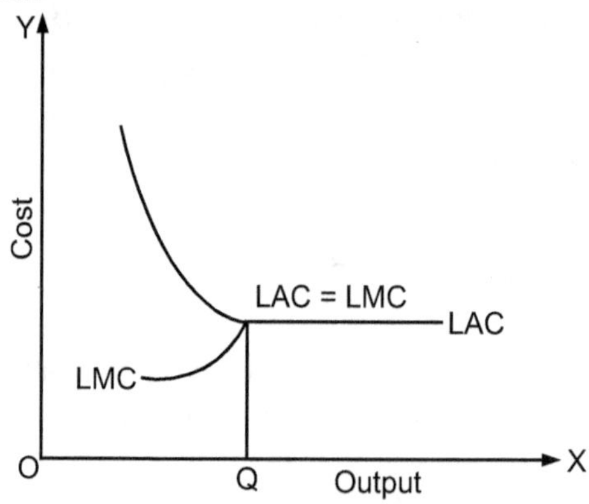

Fig. 1.11: L-shaped LAC Curve

In Fig. 1.11, LAC continues to fall till a minimum optimal scale OQ, beyond which it becomes constant indicating that the economies and diseconomies of large scale balance each other after the optimal level of output. Here, the LMC curve lies below the LAC curve until the minimum optimal scale (OQ) is reached. Thereafter, the LMC coincides with the LAC curve for higher levels of output.

1.4 REVENUE CONCEPTS

Apart from consumers, producers or sellers of goods are also very much concerned with the demand for a good, because revenues obtained by them from selling the goods, depends mainly upon the demand for the goods.

Therefore the producer is interested in knowing what sort of demand curve faces him. The demand curve of the consumers for a product is the Average Revenue (AR) curve from the standpoint of the sellers since the price paid by the consumers is revenue of the sellers.

Total Revenue (TR), Average Revenue (AR) and Marginal Revenue (MR)

1. Total Revenue (TR)

Total Revenue (TR) refers to the total amount of sales receipts received by a seller by selling a certain amount of a commodity over a period of time. The TR is obtained by multiplying the total quantity of a commodity sold by its price per unit at which it is sold.

Symbolically $TR = P \times Q$ where

TR = Total Revenue

P = Price

Q = Quantity

For instance, if the price per unit of the commodity is ₹ 50/- and if 250 units of that commodity are sold at this price, then $TR = 50 \times 250 =$ ₹ 12,500.

It is obvious that when the sales of the goods in question increase, TR increases. This shows that the slope of the TR curve is always positive. TR curve rises from left to right. Whenever it is possible to sell more and more units of the goods at a constant price (as under conditions of perfect competition), TR rises at a constant rate. In this case the TR curve is a straight line originating from the origin, TR_c in Fig. 1.12. In the case of imperfect competitions (monopoly or monopolistic competition), the firm can sell more quantity of its output only by reducing the price. Thus though TR increases with an increase in sales, the rate of increase steadily declines. Refer TR_m in Fig. 1.12.

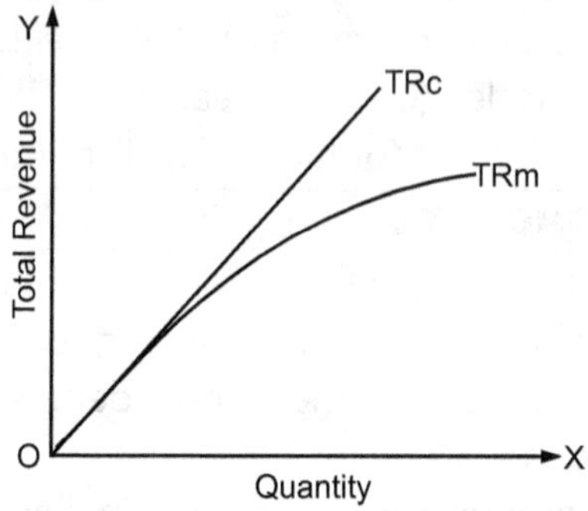

Fig. 1.12: Total Revenue Curve under Perfect Competition and Monopoly

2. Average Revenue (AR)

The price paid by the consumers for a product forms the revenue or income of the seller. The whole income received by the seller from selling a given amount of the product is called TR.

AR is revenue earned per unit of output

$$AR = \frac{TR}{Q}$$

Since
$$TR = P \times Q$$

$$AR = \frac{P \times Q}{Q}$$

$$\therefore \quad AR = \text{Price}$$

For instance, if the TR obtained by a firm selling 15 units of a commodity is ₹ 150, then

$$AR = \frac{TR}{Q} = \frac{150}{15}$$

$$\therefore \quad AR = 10$$

Since the buyer's demand curve represents graphically the quantity demanded or purchased by the buyers at various prices of the goods, it also therefore shows the AR at which the various amounts of the goods are sold by the sellers. This is because; the price paid by the buyers is revenue from the seller's point of view. Hence AR curve of the firms is really the same thing as the demand curve of the consumers.

3. Marginal Revenue (MR)

MR is the net revenue earned by selling an additional unit of the product. In other words, MR is the addition made to total revenue by selling one more unit of a commodity.

For instance, consider the following Table 1.2.

Table 1.2.

Q	TR	AR	MR
10	150	15	–
11	154	14	4

$$MR_{11} = TR_{11} - TR_{10}$$

The MR of the 11th unit (4) is the difference between the TR of the 11th unit (154) and TR of the 10th unit (150). To generalize:

$$MR_n = TR_n - TR_{n-1}$$

Marginal revenue can also be expressed as

$$MR = \frac{\Delta TR}{\Delta Q}$$

where ΔTR is change in total revenue

and ΔQ is change in quantity.

Thus marginal revenue is the change in total revenue associated with a change in quantity sold.

AR and MR under Perfect Competition

Under perfect competition, the demand curve facing an individual firm is perfectly elastic i.e. horizontal to the X-axis at the height of a given price. Under perfect competition, an individual firm cannot influence a given market price. So it is a price-taker. Since the price is beyond the control of a firm **AR remains constant** i.e. the price remains constant as more and more units are sold. So, the addition made to the TR by selling every additional unit of a commodity will always be equal to the given price. Hence **MR will also remain constant and will be equal to AR.**

For instance, consider the Table 1.3.

Table 1.3

Q (No. of units sold)	AR (Price)	TR (P × Q)	MR
1	5	5	–
2	5	10	5
3	5	15	5
4	5	20	5
5	5	25	5
6	5	30	5

The above table (Table 1.3) shows that TR increases at a constant rate as more and more units are sold. The table also shows that MR of a firm is always equal to AR or price under perfect competition.

TR, AR and MR under the conditions of perfect competition can be shown graphically as follows:

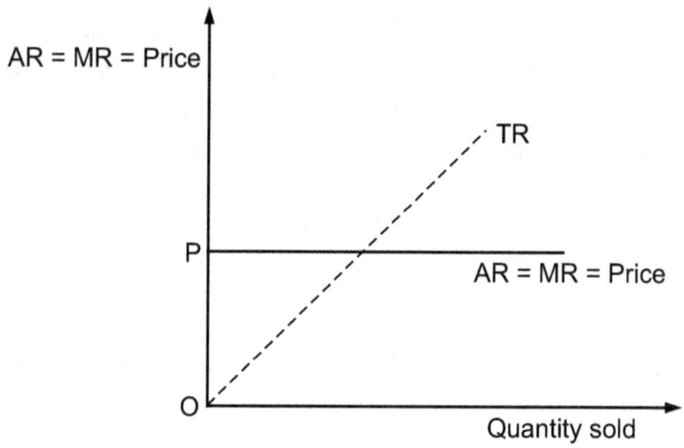

Fig. 1.13: TR, AR and MR under Perfect Competition

In the above figure (Fig. 1.13), TR moves upward to the right. Its slope is constantly positive at 45°.

AR curve in this case, is a horizontal straight line, parallel to the X-axis. The horizontal straight line or AR curve indicates that price or AR remains the same at OP level even when quantity sold is increased.

MR curve coincides with AR curve since MR = AR.

AR and MR under Imperfect Competition (Monopoly):

When imperfect competition prevails in the market for a product, an individual firm producing that product faces a downward sloping demand curve i.e. as a firm (working under conditions of imperfect competition) increases production and sale of its product, its price declines. When AR or price declines, MR also falls. So the net addition made to TR will be less than the price or AR. Hence the TR of a firm working under conditions of imperfect competition, increases at a diminishing rate. This is shown in the following Table 1.4.

Table 1.4

Output (Q)	AR or Price	TR $= AR \times Q$ $= P \times Q$	MR $= TR_n - TR_{n-1}$
0	-	0	–
1	10	10	10
2	9	18	8
3	8	24	6
4	7	28	4
5	6	30	2
6	5	30	0
7	4	28	-2
8	3	24	-4
9	2	18	-6

The above table (Table 1.4) shows that price or AR is falling as additional units of the product are sold.

MR also declines and is less than AR. TR increases at a diminishing rate. When TR is maximum, MR = 0 and when TR falls, MR < 0 (becomes negative).

AR and MR curves under conditions of imperfect competition can be shown graphically as follows:

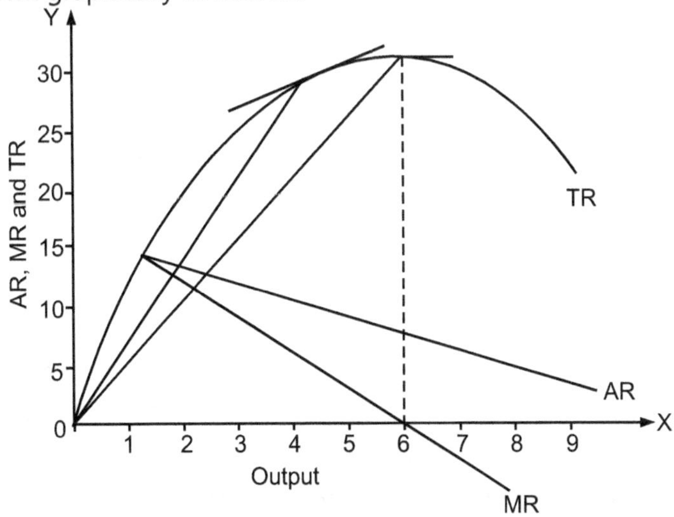

Fig. 1.14: TR, AR and MR under Imperfect Market Conditions

From the above figure (Fig. 1.14), it can be noted that in all forms of imperfect competition i.e. monopoly, monopolistic competition, olgiopoly, TR is zero, when no unit is sold. The AR curve facing an individual firm slopes downwards. When a firm lowers the price of its product, its quantity demanded and sales would increase and vice versa.

Therefore the AR curve is downward sloping and the MR curve, also downward sloping, lies below it. The fact that MR curve lies below the AR curve indicates that MR declines more rapidly than AR. When 6 units of the product are sold, MR = 0. If quantity sold is increased beyond 6, MR < 0 (-ve) i.e. TR declines.

The relationship among TR, AR, and MR can be summarized as follows:

(i) Initially, TR (i.e. price x units of the commodity sold) increases at a diminishing rate with increase in the units of output, since more units of the commodity can only be sold at a lower price, such that MR is positive and downward sloping.

(ii) When TR is maximum, MR becomes zero.

(iii) MR becomes negative, when TR decreases with increase in the units of output.

(iv) MR falls with the fall in AR, but, the rate of decrease in MR is much higher than that in AR.

(v) MR may be positive, negative or zero, but AR is always positive (since negative price is absurd).

Relationship between Total Revenue, Average Revenue and Marginal Revenue

We have seen above that when AR curve falls downward, the MR curve lies below it (or to the left of it). Now the question arises how far to the left (or below) will it lie? This will depend on the shape of the AR and MR curves.

(a) AR and MR curves are both straight line (linear demand curve) downward sloping: This is shown in Fig. 1.15.

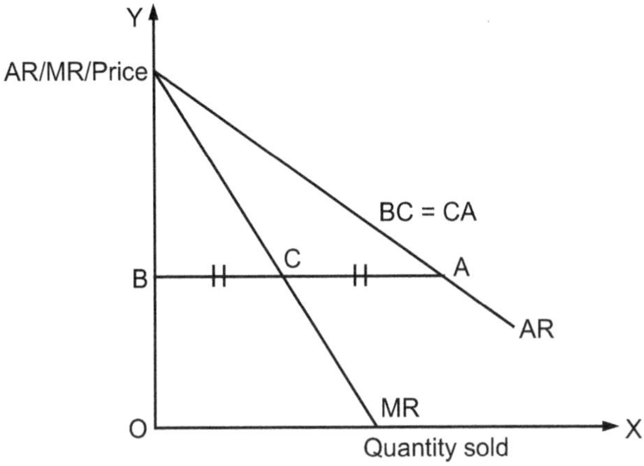

Fig. 1.15

It can be seen in the above figure (Fig. 1.15) that when AR and MR curves are both straight line downward sloping, MR curve will lie exactly halfway between the AR curve and the Y-axis i.e. the MR curve will cut the distance between the AR curve and the Y-axis in the middle i.e. MR curve will cut any perpendicular drawn from the AR curve to the Y-axis at its midpoint. Hence BC = CA.

(b) If AR curve is convex to the origin, MR curve will also be convex to the origin: This is shown in Fig. 1.16.

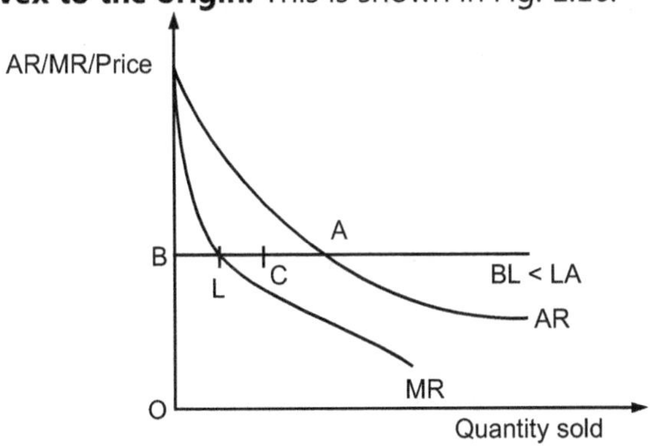

Fig. 1.16

It can be seen in the above figure (Fig. 1.16) that when AR curve is convex to the origin, MR curve will also be convex to the origin. The MR curve will cut any perpendicular drawn from AR to the Y-axis more than halfway as measured from the AR curve. I.e. MR curve cuts the perpendicular line AB at point L (which is to the left of midpoint C). Hence, BL < LA.

(c) If AR curve is concave to the origin, the MR curve will also be concave to the origin: This is shown in Fig. 1.17.

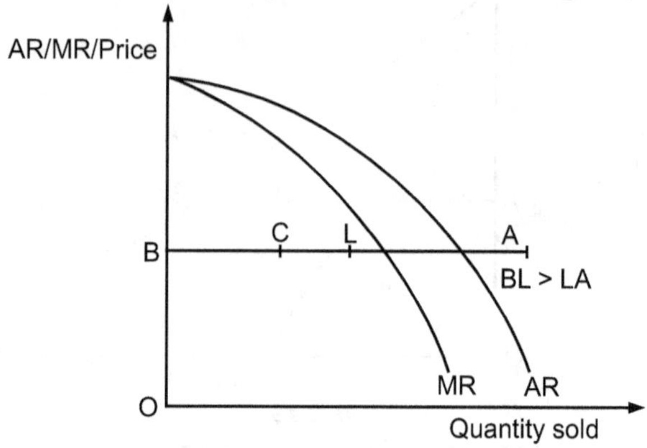

Fig. 1.17

It can be seen in the above figure (Fig. 1.17) that when AR curve is concave to the origin, the MR curve is also concave to the origin. The MR curve will cut any perpendicular drawn from AR to the Y-axis less than halfway as measured from AR curve. i.e. MR curve cuts the perpendicular line AB at point L (which is to the right of the midpoint C). Hence BL > LA.

AR, MR, TR and Elasticity of Demand

The relationship between AR, MR, TR and elasticity of demand is shown in the following figure.

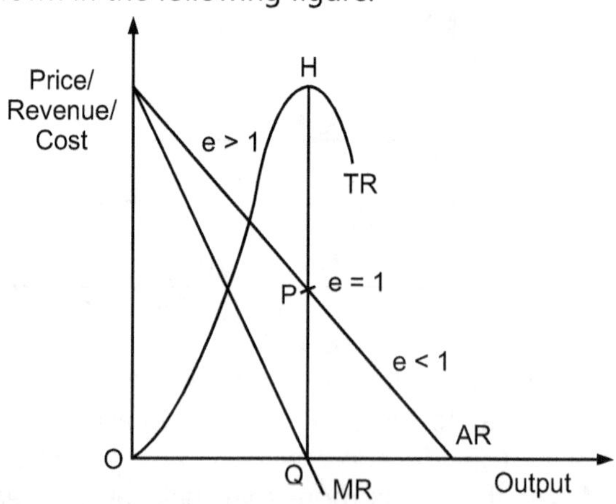

Fig. 1.18

In the above figure (Fig. 1.18) it can be seen that at OQ level of output, MR = 0, TR is maximum (at point H). Beyond OQ level of output MR < 0 (-ve), TR declines. Therefore the producer will not produce beyond OQ level of output. At point P, corresponding to OQ level of output, e = 1 (P is midpoint). Therefore the seller under **imperfect competition** will **produce and sell a level of output** which **corresponds** to the **elastic portion of his downward sloping demand curve.** If the quantity is greater than OQ, it will correspond to that portion of the AR curve where e < 1 (marginal revenue is negative, because MR goes below the X-axis). Likewise for a quantity less than OQ, e > 1 and MR is +ve. This means that if quantity greater than OQ is sold, the TR will be diminishing and for a quantity less than OQ, the TR will be increasing. Thus TR will be maximum at point H where e = 1 (unit elasticity) and MR = 0.

The relationship between AR, MR and elasticity of demand, which is extensively used in the theory of pricing can be expressed in the form of a formula:

$$e = \frac{AR}{AR - MR}, \quad MR = AR\frac{e-1}{e} \text{ and } AR = MR\frac{e}{e-1}$$

Thus for *e = 1, MR = 0. This is a very useful relationship* .Here total revenue is not affected by change in price.

Where elasticity is greater than unity, MR is positive (but, less than AR). Where elasticity is less than unity, MR is negative. It can also be observed from Fig. 4.7, that as the value of elasticity of demand increases, MR and AR curve become closer and closer to each other. The gap between them reduces to zero under perfect competition, when the demand curve is perfectly elastic.

POINTS TO REMEMBER

1. **Cost Classification:**
   (i) Historical Cost or Sunk Cost and Replacement Cost
   (ii) Private Cost and Social Cost
   (iii) Direct Cost and Indirect Cost
   (iv) Real Cost and Actual Cost
   (v) Opportunity Cost or Alternative Cost

(vi) Incremental and Marginal Cost
(vii) Accounting Cost and Economic Cost
(viii) Opportunity Cost, Economic Cost and Accounting Cost

2. **Behaviour of Cost Curves:** A firm's cost functions will vary, depending on whether they are based on the **short run period** or **long run period.** Here 'period' or 'time' refers to the functional or operational time period. Short run and long run do not refer to any calendar time. They are sets of conditions and not periods of time. A short run period is one during which certain factors like factory buildings, number of machines, land, managerial staff etc remain fixed. Hence these factors are called **fixed factors.** So, in a short run period, the size of the plant of a firm and its scale of production would remain constant. However in the short run, the other factors such as labour, raw materials and power can be varied in amount. Hence these factors are called **variable factors.**

   A **long run period** is one during which all the factors of production can be fully varied in amount by a firm i.e. in the long run, all the factors become variable. So, in the long run, the size of the plant of a firm and its scale of production can be fully increased or decreased.

3. **Short Run Costs:**
   (a) Total Fixed Cost (TFC)
   (b) Total Variable Cost (TVC)
   (c) Total Cost (TC)- TC=TFC+TVC
   (d) Average Fixed Cost (AFC)
   (e) Average Variable Cost (AVC)
   (f) Average total cost (ATC) or Average Cost (AC)
   (g) Marginal Cost (MC)

4. **Long Run Costs:**
   (a) Long run Average Cost (LAC)
   (b) Long run Marginal Cost (LMC)

5. **Total Revenue (TR)** refers to the total amount of sales receipts received by a seller by selling a certain amount of a commodity over a period of time. The TR is obtained by multiplying the total quantity of a commodity sold by its price per unit at which it is sold.

   Symbolically $TR = P \times Q$

6. The price paid by the consumers for a product forms the revenue or income of the seller. The whole income received by the seller from selling a given amount of the product is called TR.

   AR is revenue earned per unit of output

$$AR = \frac{TR}{Q}$$

   Marginal Revenue is the net revenue earned by selling an additional unit of the product. In other words, MR is the addition made to total revenue by selling one more unit of a commodity.

   Marginal revenue can be expressed as:

$$MR = \frac{\Delta TR}{\Delta Q}$$

   where ΔTR is change in total revenue

   and ΔQ is change in quantity.

QUESTIONS FOR DISCUSSION

1. Distinguish between:
   (a) Historical Cost and Replacement Cost
   (b) Direct Cost and Indirect Cost
   (c) Incremental Cost and Marginal Cost
   (d) Accounting concept of cost and Economic concept of cost.
2. Explain the concept of Opportunity Cost.
3. Distinguish between short run and long run period.
4. Define Total Cost. What are the components of Total Cost?
5. Explain the behaviour of TC, TFC and TVC.
6. Define Average Cost. What are the components of Average Cost?
7. Define Marginal Cost.
8. Explain the relationship between AC and MC.
9. Define and explain the Long-run average cost.
10. Why is the LAC called an 'envelope curve?
11. Why is the LAC curve U shaped?
12. What do empirical investigations suggest about the LAC curves?

13. Describe the Total Revenue Curve under perfect competition and under monopoly.
14. Show how AR = Price.
15. Why is the AR curve of the firm the same thing as the demand curve of the customers?
16. Define Marginal Revenue. How can we derive MR from TR?
17. Describe the relationship between AR and MR under perfect competition.
18. Describe the relationship between AR and MR under imperfect competition?
19. Establish the relationship between MR, AR and elasticity of demand.

QUESTIONS FROM PAST EXAMINATIONS

1. What is Opportunity Cost? **[April 2009, Oct. 2009]**
2. Define Marginal Cost. **[Oct. 2010]**
3. What are the various Types of Costs? **[April 2010]**
4. What is Marginal Revenue? **[April 2009, Oct. 2009, April 2010]**
5. What is Total Revenue? **[Oct. 2010]**
6. State concepts of Total Revenue, Average Revenue and Marginal Revenue. **[Oct. 2012]**
7. State the concept of Total Revenue, Average Revenue and Marginal Revenue. **[April 2014, 2018, Oct. 2015, 2016, 2017]**
8. State the Importance of Revenue Concept **[April 2015]**
9. Write Short Notes: Concept of TR, AR, MR **[April 2016]**

■■■

Unit **2**...

Pricing Under Perfect Market Conditions

Contents ...

Learning Objectives ...

- To discuss the concept of Pure Competition
- To deliberate on the features of Perfect Competition
- To learn about price determination in Perfect Competition
- To understand the equilibrium of firm and industry in Short Run and Long Run

INTRODUCTION

The theory of demand provides an explanation of the consumer's behaviour in order to deduce the demand for a commodity. Similarly, the theory of firm explains the goals and objectives of a firm (through the behaviour of firm) and together enable us to ascertain the price and output of a commodity or service by the free interplay of the forces of demand and supply in the market. The nature of the demand curve and the price-output business decisions depend upon the type of the market in which the commodity is produced and sold. In Economics, the term market does not refer to any particular market place in which things are bought and sold, but to a set of conditions in which buyers and sellers interact with one another for the purpose of exchange at an agreed price.

The important elements of a market are discussed below:

1. **Nature of the product,** which is being bought and sold in the market at a price mutually agreeable to both. The closer the substitutes available for a product, the greater is the competition in the market.
2. **Number of firms** *(sellers)* or *size of the industry.*
3. **Existence of competition** *among* the *buyers and sellers,* as a result of an increase in their number. Competition among the buyers raises the price, while competition among the sellers results in a fall in the price. Awareness and mobility positively affect the competition in the market.
4. **Free communication** between the buyers and sellers so that the price between different buyers and sellers is the same.
5. **The place** where the commodity is traded. It can be a certain city, a region, a country or even the world.
6. **Government policies** about liberalisation, price control, location of production, choice of technology, taxes, subsidies, foreign trade policies etc.

Markets may be classified:

(a) On the basis of **area** as **local, national** and **world** markets;

(b) On the basis of **time,** as **market price** on any particular day or moment, **short-period price, long-period price or secular markets;**

(c) On the basis of nature of **competition** obtaining therein as **perfect markets** and **imperfect markets.**

Market Forms or Market Structures: In discussing market structures, we concentrate on the third basis of classification mentioned above. The popular basis of classifying market structures rests on two crucial elements:

(a) The number of firms producing a product,

(b) The nature of the product produced by the firms i.e. whether it is homogeneous or differentiated. A distinguishing feature of different market categories is the degree of price elasticity of demand faced by an individual firm.

Classification of Market Forms

Form of Market Structure	Number of Firms	Nature of Product	P_{ed} for an Individual Firm	Degree of Control over Price
(a) Prefect or Pure Competition	A large number of firms	Homogeneous product	Infinite	None
(b) Imperfect Competition				
(i) Monopolistic Competition	A large number of firms	Differentiated products (close substitutes of each other)	Large	Some
(ii) Duopoly (Pure or differentiated)	Two	Homogeneous or Differentiated	Low	Some
(iii) Pure Oligopoly (No product differentiation)	Few firms	Homogeneous product	Small	Some
(iv) Differentiated monopoly	Few firms	Differentiated products (close substitutes)	Small	Large
(c) Monopoly	One	Unique product without close substitute	Very small	Very large

Perfect competition and monopoly are the two extremes of the market situations. Monopolistic competition and oligopoly fall in between these two extremes.

2.1 PURE COMPETITION

Pure competition is said to exist when the following conditions are fulfilled.

1. **Large number of buyers and sellers:** Presence of a large number of buyers and sellers prevents any single producer or buyer to wield an influence in the market. The output of any single firm is only a small portion of the total output and the

demand of any particular purchaser is only a small part of the market. Hence, the market price has to be taken as given and unalterable by every purchaser and seller. Thus, no individual purchaser can influence the market price by varying his own demand and no single firm is in a position to affect the market price by varying its output. Therefore, every firm is a price taker (not a price maker) and can sell as much as it can produce at the prevailing market price.

2. **Homogeneous product:** The second condition is that the output produced by all the firms should be uniform and standardised in all respects. In such a case, it would be immaterial for the purchaser to know as to who has produced it. He would be able to buy from any seller in the market without any prejudices. Since the products are perfect substitutes for one another, the cross elasticity of demand is infinite. In these circumstances, if a firm raises its price, it will lose all the customers. No firm would like to lower the price below the prevailing level, as it can sell any quantity at the prevailing price. Since the price of the commodity remains constant at its prevailing level, all the units of the commodity must be sold at the same price.

2.2 PERFECT COMPETITION

Perfect Competition is a wider term than pure competition. In addition to the above two conditions of pure competition, several other conditions must be fulfilled to make a market a perfectly competitive one. Usually, the term pure competition and perfect competition are used interchangeably, (American economists prefer to use the term pure competition, while the term perfect competition is popular with the British economists) since in both cases sellers as well as buyers are price takers with no control over the prevailing market price. Further, the demand and supply curves of the firms as well as industry are similar in either situations.

1. **Free entry or exit:** There should be no restrictions, legal, technological, financial or any other barriers to the entry of firms into the industry. Similarly existing firms have freedom to quit the industry. In this situation, all the firms will be making just normal profits. (Normal profit is the opportunity cost of the entrepreneur i.e. the minimum amount necessary to attract him to an activity or to induce him to remain in it.) If the profit is

more than normal (super normal profits), new firms will enter and the extra profit will be competed away. If, on the other hand, profit is less than normal (losses), some firms will quit the industry, raising the profits to the normal level for the remaining firms. Thus freedom of entry or exit maintains the profits at normal profit level.

2. **Perfect mobility of factors of production:** Mobility of the factors of production enables the firms to adjust their supply to demand. If the demand exceeds supply, price for the factor increases and additional factors would be attracted into the industry and this increase in supply would lower the price to the equilibrium level. On the other hand, when supply exceeds demand, prices fall; some factors move out of the industry and the fall in supply pulls up the price to the equilibrium level. Thus mobility of factors of production is essential to enable the firms and industry to achieve an equilibrium position.
3. **Perfect knowledge of market conditions:** Another assumption of perfect competition is that the buyers and sellers should be fully aware of the prices that are being offered and accepted. In case there is ignorance among the dealers, the same price cannot rule in the market for the same commodity. When the producers and customers have full knowledge of the prevailing price, no seller can sell at a higher price than the other and no buyer can buy the output at a lower price than the other. Given the price, the producers can sell any amount and the buyers can buy as much as they like.
4. **Absence of transport cost:** If the same price is to rule in the market, it is necessary that no cost of transport is incurred or if it is incurred it should be the same for the entire market. This is because differences in cost of transport would result in different prices in different sectors of the market.
5. **Absence of Government Regulation:** There is no restraint upon the independence of the buyer and seller. Any type of government intervention into the free interplay of market forces is assumed to be absent. Thus the intervention of the Government through tariffs, taxes, subsidies, duties is ruled out.

In the words of Prof. Boulding, "a perfectly competitive market may be defined as a large number of buyers and sellers, all engaged in the purchase and sale of identically similar commodities, who are in close contact with one another and who buy and sell freely among themselves."

Perfect competition is an 'ideal' concept of market rather than an actual market reality. To some extent, the perfect competitive model fits into the market for farm products like rice, cotton, wheat etc.

2.3 PRICE AND OUTPUT DETERMINATION UNDER PERFECT COMPETITION– SHAPE OF THE DEMAND CURVE UNDER PERFECT COMPETITION

Average Revenue (AR) is the revenue per unit of the commodity sold. AR means price. The consumer's demand curve is the graphic relation between price and amount demanded. It also represents the AR or price at which the various amounts of the commodity are sold. Further, the price offered by the buyer is the revenue from the seller's point of view. Therefore AR curve of the firm is the same thing as the demand curve of the consumer.

In the case of perfect competition, the marginal revenue (MR) is also equal to AR (price) because additional units are sold at the same price. The seller under perfect competition can sell any amount of the commodity at the ruling market price. This is because no individual firm has the power to vary the market price (since the number of firms is very large). Besides, the products are identical from the consumer's point of view. Hence the price paid by them cannot be different. This is represented as follows:

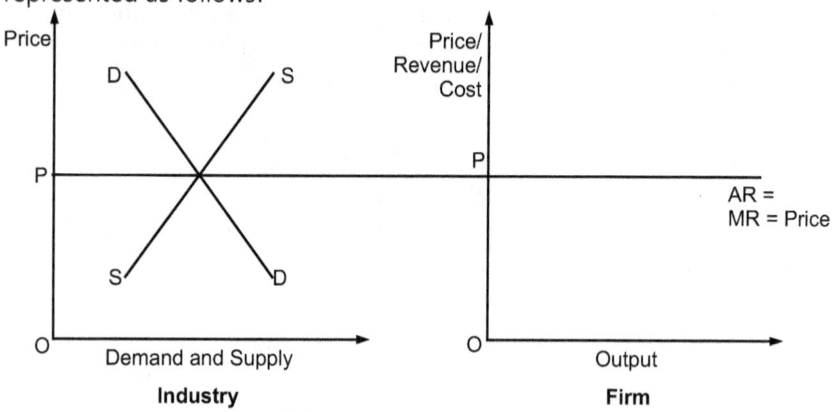

Fig. 2.1

In the above (Fig. 2.1) it is seen that the firm is a price taker. MR=AR. The demand curve **(AR curve)** is **perfectly elastic.** At price OP (determined by market forces of demand and supply) the firm can sell as much as it can produce.

Equilibrium of a Firm

A firm is in equilibrium when it earns maximum profits. Total profits can be increased by expanding output as long as the addition to revenue resulting from the sale of extra unit of output is greater than the addition to cost caused by producing an extra output. The addition to total revenue (TR) and total cost (TC) due to an extra unit of output are nothing else but MR and MC respectively. Thus a firm goes on expanding output as long as MR exceeds MC of production. The level of output where the MR and MC are equal is the point of maximum profit. This equality is a necessary condition but not a sufficient condition of equilibrium. For attaining equilibrium, a second condition must also be satisfied i.e. the MC must cut the MR curve from below. In other words, beyond the equilibrium output MC must be greater than MR. If this condition is not met, a firm will not be earning maximum profits and hence will not be in equilibrium. Thus for a **firm to be in equilibrium position, (under any market condition), two conditions must be satisfied:**

(i) Necessary Condition: MC = MR and

(ii) Sufficient Condition: MC curve must cut MR curve from below at equilibrium output.

These two conditions hold good both in the short run as well as in the long run. The only difference is that in the short run it is the short run MC curve and in the long run it is the long run MC curve which is relevant for comparing with MR curve.

Under perfect competition, a firm is in equilibrium when the above two conditions are satisfied. This can be illustrated in the following diagram:

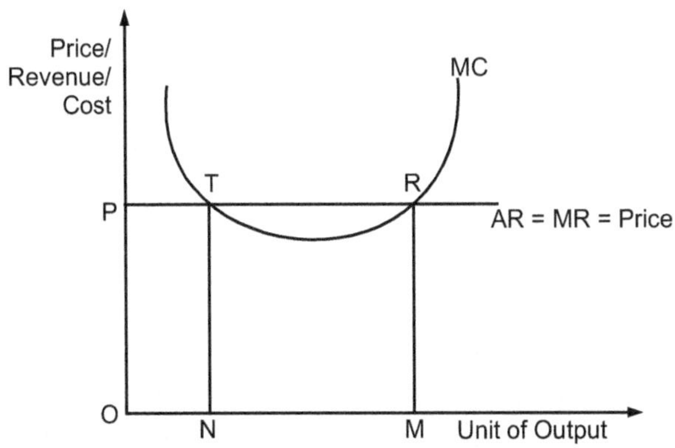

Fig. 2.2: Conditions for Equilibrium under Perfect Competition

In the above Fig. 2.2, the demand curve is represented by the horizontal line parallel to the X-axis. The price at which the output is sold is OP. The demand curve (AR) also represents the MR curve. At point T, MC is equal to MR but MC cuts MR from above. Therefore T cannot be a position of equilibrium. Expansion of output beyond ON would be profitable for the firm because the MC is less than MR. The firm would increase its output till the level OM. At this level MC cuts the MR curve from below at point R. Here the profits would be maximum. Expansion of output beyond level OM would be unprofitable as MC is greater than MR. Hence at point R, the two conditions namely (i) MC = MR and (ii) MC curve cuts MR curve from below are satisfied.

2.4 (A) SHORT RUN EQUILIBRIUM OF A FIRM UNDER PERFECT COMPETITION

The short run has been defined as a period of time sufficient to allow the firm to adjust its output by increasing or decreasing the amount of variable factors of production, but during which fixed factors of production cannot be altered. Thus, in the short run, the size and kind of plant cannot be changed, nor can new firms enter the industry.

In explaining the equilibrium of a firm under perfect competition both in the short run and long run, we assume that all firms are working under **identical cost conditions** (i.e. AC and MC curves are identical for all firms).

The above twin conditions of equilibrium (MC = MR and MC must cut the MR curve from below) ensure that profits have been maximised or losses minimised, but they do not tell about the firm's absolute profit or loss position. In this connection there are three possibilities:

(i) When the firm makes **supernormal profits** (where AR > AC, which also implies TR > TC: any profit over and above normal profit.

(ii) When the firm makes **normal profits** (where AR = AC, which also implies TR = TC): that amount of earnings which is sufficient to induce the firm to stay in the industry or the minimum level of profit which the entrepreneur must get such that he continues to employ resources in its present occupation or the least possible reward earned by the entrepreneur as compensation for his organisational services and for bearing business risks. Normal profits are always included in the cost of production.

(iii) When the firm **incurs losses**, but still does not shut down (where AR < AC, which also implies TR < TC).

(i) Case of Super normal profits: (AR > AC; TR > TC)

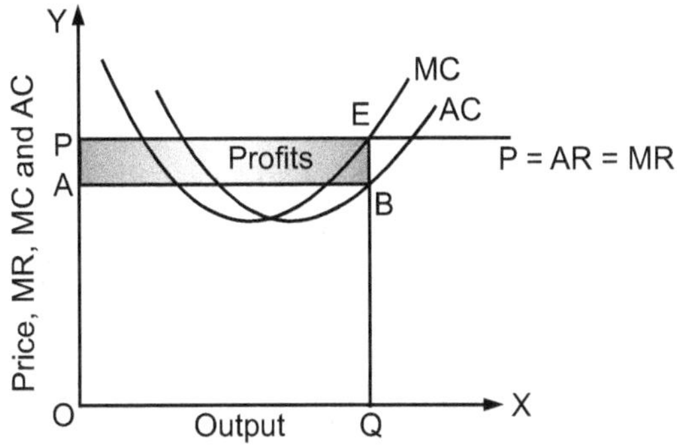

Fig. 2.3: Case of Super Normal Profits (SNP)

In the above Fig. 2.3, if the price is OP, the MC curve cuts MR curve from below at point E and the firm produces OQ output. The AC curve being below the AR curve, the firm makes SNP per unit of output of EB [AR = EQ; AC = BQ since EQ > BQ, per unit of output SNP = EB]. For output OQ, the firm makes SNP equal to the area APEB.

$$
\begin{aligned}
[\text{TR} &= \text{AR} \times \text{output} \\
&= \text{EQ} \times \text{OQ} = \text{OPEQ} \\
\text{TC} &= \text{AC} \times \text{output} \\
&= \text{BQ} \times \text{OQ} = \text{OABQ} \\
\text{TR} &> \text{TC. Hence SNP} = \text{APEB.]}
\end{aligned}
$$

When the firm makes SNP, there will be a tendency for new firms to enter the industry to compete away these SNPs. But the short run is not a period sufficient for new firms to enter; therefore the existing firm will continue to earn SNP at the price OP in the short period.

(ii) Case of Normal Profits (AR = AC; TR = TC):

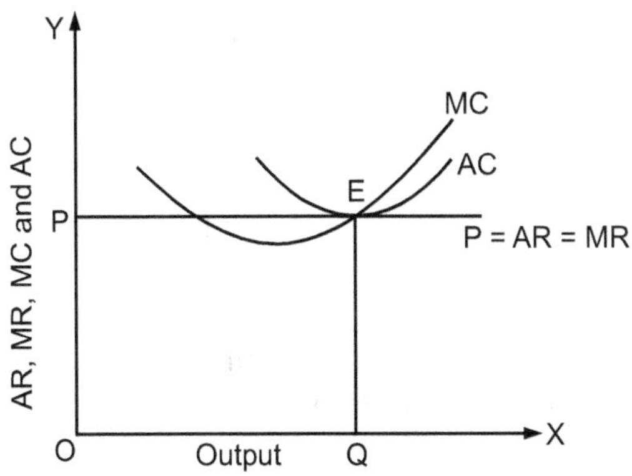

Fig. 2.4: Case of Normal Profits

In the above Fig. 2.4, at price OP, the firm is in equilibrium at point E producing output OQ. At point E, AR is also equal to AC. Hence the firm makes normal profits. [AR = EQ and AC = EQ]. Hence, normal profits.

$$[\,R = EQ \times OQ = OPEQ$$
$$TC = EQ \times OQ = OPEQ$$
$$TR = TC\text{, Hence normal profit}].$$

(iii) Case of Losses (AR < AC; TR < TC), but firm does not shut down.

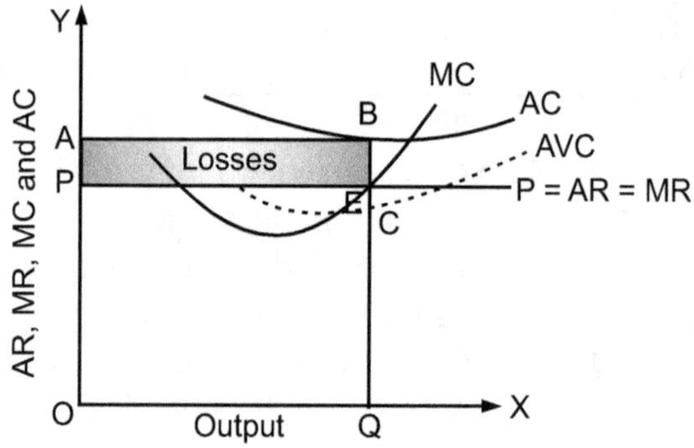

Fig. 2.5: Case of Losses

In the above Fig. 2.5, at price OP the firm is in equilibrium at point E producing OQ output. The AC curve being above the AR curve, the firm incurs loss per unit of output of BE. [AR = EQ; AC = BQ. Since EQ < BQ, loss per unit of output = BE]. For output OQ, the firm incurs loss equal to the area PABE.

$$[TR = EQ \times OQ = OPEQ$$
$$TC = BQ \times OQ = OABQ$$
$$TR < TC\text{. Hence loss} = PABE]$$

When the firm incurs losses, there will be a tendency for the firm to leave the industry. But it cannot do so in the short run.

The question, which arises is, why the firms should continue operating if they are incurring losses; if they cannot leave the industry, why do they not at least shut down to avoid losses.

The short run is a period in which the firms cannot alter their fixed capital equipment. Therefore they will have to bear the fixed costs in the short run even if they shut down. Only, variable cost can be avoided by stopping production. Therefore, if the firm chooses to shut down in the short run, even then it will have to bear losses equal to the fixed cost of production.

Hence, if the firm in operation can earn **revenue more than the variable cost,** it will not be prudent for the firm to close merely because it is not possible to cover fixed costs fully. Instead, **the firm should keep operating in the short run, if it can cover variable costs and make anything to cover a part of the fixed costs also.** But if the price happens to be so low that the firm cannot cover even its variable costs, it should shut down in order to minimise the losses.

Shut-down point: If losses are greater than total fixed costs, i.e. when revenue earned is even less than the total variable costs, the firm will shut down to avoid unnecessary losses. The whole argument can be understood with the help of the following diagram.

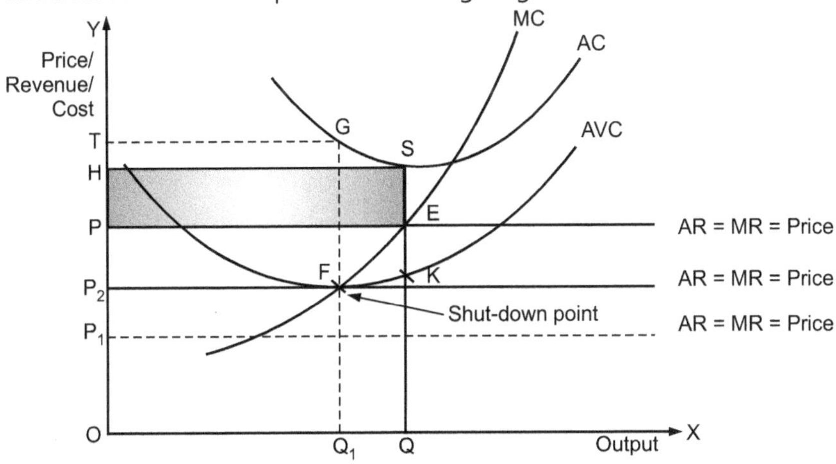

Fig. 2.6: Equilibrium of a firm in the Short Run - Shut down point

In the above Fig. 2.6, when price is OP the firm is in equilibrium at E and incurs a loss of PESH, but the firm covers total variable cost and a part the fixed costs, since AR or price OP (=EQ) is greater than average variable cost KQ at the equilibrium output OQ. Hence, in the short run, it is in the interest of the firm to keep operating at price OP.

But if the price happens to fall to OP_2, the firm will be in equilibrium at F and incurs a loss of P_2FGT. At point F the firm covers total variable cost but no part of the fixed costs, since AR or price OP_2 (= FQ_1) is also equal to average variable cost FQ_1 at the equilibrium output OQ_1. The firm does not cover any part of the fixed cost at the output level OQ_1. But if the price is less than OP_2 (= FQ_1) i.e. if price is less than the bottom of Average Variable Cost, the firm would shut down, as in that situation it would not cover even the variable costs, since the price will be less than the average variable cost. Point F is therefore called the shut down point.

For example, at price OP_1, the firm would not cover even variable cost since OP_1 is less than the AVC at every level of output. With price OP_1 the firm's losses would be equal to fixed costs plus a part of the variable cost not covered by the total revenue. Therefore, the firm will refuse to produce any output at price OP_1 and wait for some good time to re-open.

Hence it can be concluded that a firm will shut down in the short run, if the price falls below the bottom of the AVC curve.

(B) LONG RUN EQUILIBRIUM OF A FIRM UNDER PERFECT COMPETITION

The long run is a period of time long enough to permit changes in the variable as well as in the fixed factors. Accordingly, in the long run firms can change their output by increasing their fixed equipments. They can enlarge the old plants or replace them by new plants or add new plants. Moreover, in the long run, new firms can also enter the industry. On the contrary, if the situation so demands, in the long run, existing firms can leave the industry.

Thus the long run equilibrium of a firm refers to a situation where free and full scope for adjustment is allowed. In the long run it is the long run average (LAC) and marginal cost (LMC) curves which are relevant for making output decisions. In the long run, for a perfectly competitive firm to be in equilibrium, besides MC being equal to MR (AR or Price), price (AR) must also be equal to LAC (at its minimum point). If price (AR) is greater than LAC, the firms will be making SNPs. Attracted by these SNP; new firms will enter the industry to compete away these profits. When new firms enter the industry, the supply of output of the industry will increase and hence the price of the output will be forced down. The new firms will keep coming into the industry until the price is supressed down to AC and all firms are earning only normal profits.

On the other hand if the price (AR) happens to be below LAC, the firm will be incurring losses. Some of the existing firms will quit the industry. As a result, the output of the industry will decrease and the price will rise to equal LAC so that the firms remaining in the industry are making normal profits.

Thus, for a perfectly competitive firm to be in equilibrium in the long run, the following two conditions must be satisfied: P = LMC and P = LAC. If price (AR) equals both LMC and LAC then for long run equilibrium of the firm under perfect competition, we have a combined condition.

Price (AR) or MR = LMC = LAC (at its minimum point). This can be diagrammatically illustrated as follows:

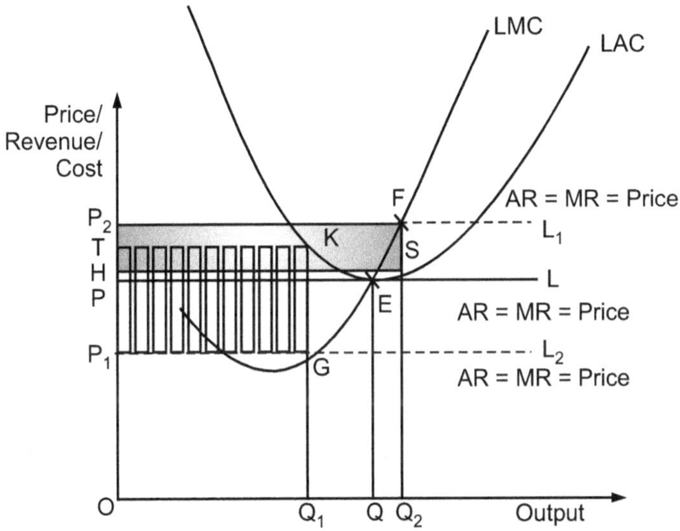

Fig. 2.7: Equilibrium of a firm in the Long Run

In the above Fig. 2.7, LAC is the long run average cost curve and LMC is the long run marginal cost curve. The firm under perfect competition cannot be in equilibrium at price OP_2 because although price OP_2 equals LMC at F (output OQ_2), but it is greater than LAC at this output and therefore the firm will be earning SNP of P_2FSH. Since all the firms are assumed to be identical, all would be earning SNPs. Hence there will incentive for the new firms to enter the industry. As a result, output would increase and the price would be forced down to the level OP at which price, the firm is in equilibrium at E and is producing OQ output. At point E or equilibrium output OQ the price (AR) = LAC and hence the firm will be earning only normal profits. Hence at price OP there will be no tendency for new firms to enter.

On the contrary, a firm under perfect competition cannot be in long run equilibrium at price OP_1. Though price OP_1 = LMC at point G or at output OQ_1, but the price OP_1 (AR) is lower than LAC and the firm will be incurring losses of P_1GKT. To avoid these losses, some of the firms will leave the industry. As a result output shrinks and price will rise to OP where again all firms make normal profits.

Thus, we conclude that at price OP the firm under perfect compete-tion is in equilibrium in the long run when Price (AR) or MR = LMC = LAC (at its minimum point).

(C) EQUILIBRIUM OF THE INDUSTRY IN THE LONG RUN UNDER PERFECT COMPETITION

In the long run an industry would be in equilibrium when every firm enjoys only **normal profits.** This would be the case when the following conditions are fulfilled.

(i) LMR of every firm is equal to its LMC.

(ii) The LMC curve of every firm cuts its LMR curve from below.

(iii) LAR of every firm is equal to its LAC.

When LAR = LAC, the number of firms in the industry would remain constant and the industry would attain equilibrium.

When LAR > LAC the existing firms would enjoy SNP. This would induce new firms to enter the industry; the output would increase and the price would come down until it is equal to LAC.

On the other hand when LAR < LAC, the existing firms would suffer losses. This would force some of them to leave it. Hence the output would decrease and the price would rise until it becomes equal to LAC. This can be illustrated as follows:

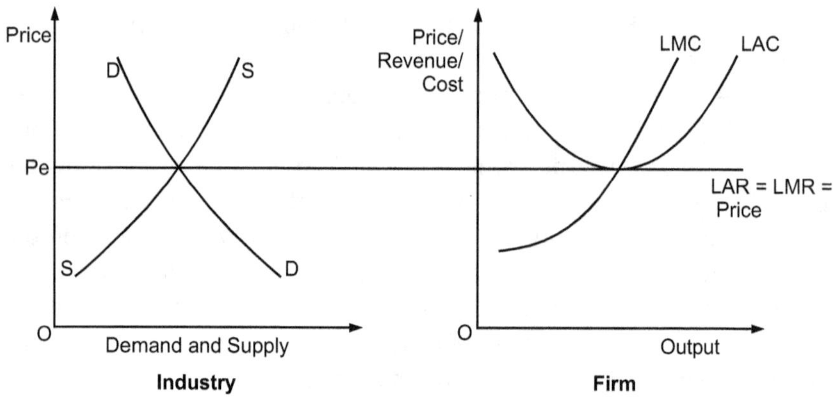

Fig. 2.8

The equilibrium price P_e is set when LAR = LMR = LAC (at its minimum point) = LMC.

Hence at the above condition, the number of firms in the industry is stable as no entry of new firms or exit of existing firms takes place. All firms earn only normal profits.

Short Run Supply Curve of a Competitive Firm

As discussed under the short-run equilibrium of a perfectly competitive firm, a firm under perfect competition keeps operating in the short run, so long as it is able to cover at least its variable costs. Thus, a firm which is not in a position to cover its short run variable costs will choose to shut down its business. By doing so, the competitive firm minimizes its losses in the short run.

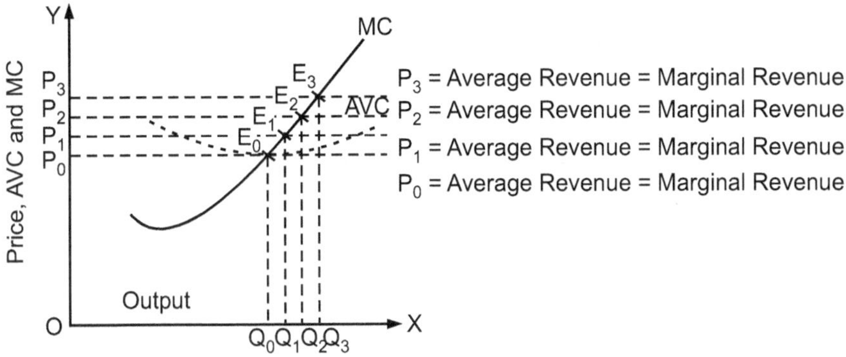

Fig. 2.9 Short-run Supply Curve of a Competitive Firm

The point at which the firm just covers its variable costs of production is called *shut-down point or closing down point.* With U-shaped cost curves, it is at the minimum point of the average variable cost. The concept of shut-down point can be used to derive the supply curve of a competitive firm in the short run. This is illustrated in Fig. 2.9.

In the Fig. 2.9, it can be seen that, if the market price is OP_0, the firm will supply an output of OQ_0 and operate at equilibrium point $E_{0.}$, where MC is equal to MR. Similarly when the price rises to OP_1, the firm will supply an equilibrium output of OQ_1. Further when the price rises to OP_2, the firm raises the supply to OQ_2. Likewise the firm supplies OQ3 output at OP_3 price.

OP_0 is the minimum acceptable price in this short run for the firm under consideration, below which the firm stops production. At this price, only variable costs are covered. The corresponding equilibrium point E_0 is the shut down point of the firm, where price (P) = minimum of AVC and TR = TVC. As the market price increases gradually, the firm confronts new demand curves at higher and higher levels. With positive slope of the MC curve, each higher demand curve (AR = MR) cuts the given MC curve at a point, which lies to the right of the previous intersection. This means that the quantity supplied by the firm along its MC curve increases as price rises in the short run. The horizontal co-ordinate of a point on the rising

MC curve measures the quantity of product that the firm will supply at that price. Thus, the MC curve of the firm indicates the quantities of output which the firm will supply at various prices.

It is important to note that the competitive firm's short run supply curve is identical with only that portion of the short-run MC curve, which lies above the AVC curve. It is derived by joining the points of intersection of the MC curve with the successive individual demand curves, as the market price of the product keeps rising above the AVC. The quantity supplied by the firm is equal to zero at all prices less than those corresponding to the shut- down point. The firm's supply curve is shown by the dark segment in Fig. 2.9. (from point E_0 upwards)

Long Run Supply Curve of a Competitive Firm

The derivation of long run supply curve of a competitive firm is similar to the derivation of its short-run supply curve. This is shown in Fig. 2.10 by dark segments.

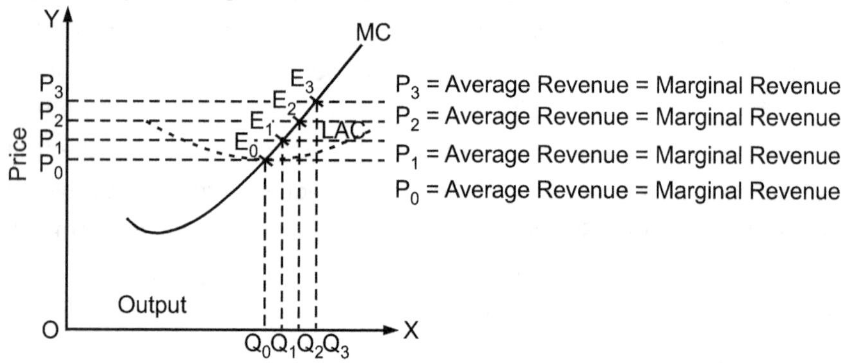

Fig. 2.10: Long-run Supply Curve of a Competitive Firm

The firm's long-run optimal output corresponding to different price levels is determined by the equality of price (AR = MR) and the long run marginal cost (LMC). Zero output is produced at prices less than the long: run average cost (LAC). In Fig. 2.10, OP_0 is the minimum acceptable price in the long run. At this price, the competitive firm attains equilibrium at point E_0 and supplies OQ_0 output. At price OP_1, equilibrium is attained at point E_1 with OQ_1 as the output produced. Further, at OP_2 price, the output supplied is OQ_2, while the output supplied is OQ_3 at OP_3 price and so on. All equilibrium points, such as E_0, E_1, E_2 and E_3 lie on the firm's

LMC curve. These points also show the supply curve of the competitive firm in the long-run at various prices. Therefore, the portion of LMC curve of the competitive firm above its LAC curve is its long run supply curve. Long: run supply curve of a perfectly competitive firm, is thus, and derived by joining together the points of intersection of the LMC curve with the successive demand curves of the firm, as the market price of the product under consideration keeps rising above its average cost.

Perfect Competition - Myth or Reality?

Does perfect competition exist in the real world?

The features of a perfectly competitive market are rarely found to exist together in any real market. For example, it is difficult to find a **perfectly homogeneous** product; most real life products have some degree of differentiation like brand name and even packaging. Similarly, **perfect knowledge** despite widespread advance in communication technology, perfect information is still not very common in all industries.

Hence, perfect competition is not a common phenomenon in the real world. In perfect competition, as such, firms do not compete with each other; they accept whatever price prevails and adjust their supplies accordingly. An individual firm cannot even make a negligible effect on the market. In such circumstances, one wonders whether there is any competition at all.

It is the agricultural market that probably comes closest to exhibiting **almost** all the features of perfect competition. It is characterized by many small producers/farmers who do not have the ability to command the selling price of their products. There exists knowledge (though not perfect) about the product and its price in the market. Entry and exit from the market is also easy. Stock market, bullion market and market for petroleum products comes close to fit all the features of the perfect competition.

Despite the fact that perfect competition is a rarity in real life, it still finds great relevance in economic theory, especially as it is the **most efficient and ideal form** of market. This market ensures that all economic resources are put to productive use and that a market economy in its true sense prevails only in perfect competition.

POINTS TO REMEMBER

1. The important **elements of a market:**
   - (a) Nature of the product
   - (b) Number of firms (sellers) or size of the industry
   - (c) Existence of competition among the buyers and sellers
   - (d) Free communication between the buyers and sellers
   - (e) The place where the commodity is traded
   - (f) Government policies
2. **Markets may be classified:**
   - (a) On the basis of area as local, national and world markets;
   - (b) On the basis of time, as market price on any particular day or moment, short-period price, long-period price or secular markets;
   - (c) On the basis of nature of competition obtaining therein as perfect markets and imperfect markets.
3. **Perfect competition** is said to exist when the following conditions are fulfilled.
   - (a) Large number of buyers and sellers
   - (b) Homogeneous product
   - (c) Free entry or exit
   - (d) Perfect mobility of factors of production
   - (e) Perfect knowledge of market conditions
   - (f) Absence of transport costs
   - (g) Absence of government regulation
4. **Equilibrium of a firm:** A firm is in equilibrium when it earns maximum profits.
5. Firm to be in equilibrium position, (under any market condition), two conditions must be satisfied:
   - (i) Necessary Condition: MC = MR and
   - (ii) Sufficient Condition: MC curve must cut MR curve from below at equilibrium output.
6. **Short-run equilibrium of a firm under perfect competition**
   - (a) Super Normal Profits (SNP) where AR > AC.

(b) Losses where AR < AC.

(c) Normal Profits (NP) where AR = AC.

7. Long-run equilibrium of a firm under perfect competition

   (Price) AR = MR = LMC = LAC.

8. **Equilibrium of industry:** It is the equilibrium of all firms in the industry.

   In the long run - LAR = LMR = LAC (at its minimum point) = LMC.

9. **Perfect competition** is the most efficient and ideal form of market.

QUESTIONS FOR DISCUSSION

1. What is a market? How are markets classified?
2. Distinguish between Pure Competition and Perfect Competition.
3. What is Perfect Competition? What are its features or characteristics or conditions?
4. Describe the demand curve under perfect competition.
5. What are the conditions of equilibrium of a firm under any market structure?
6. Describe the short run equilibrium of a firm under perfect competition.
7. Describe the shut down point of a firm under perfect competition.
8. Describe the long run equilibrium of a firm under perfect competition.
9. Describe the equilibrium of the industry in the long run under perfect competition.
10. Explain the derivation of short-run supply curve of a competitive firm.
11. Explain the derivation of long- run supply curve of a competitive firm.

QUESTIONS FROM PAST EXAMINATIONS

1. Explain short-run Equilibrium of a Firm under Perfect Competition. **[Oct. 2009, April 2009]**
2. Explain Equilibrium of a Firm and Industry in the short and long run period under Perfect Competition. **[April 2010]**

3. What is Perfect Competition? Explain Short-run and long-run Equilibrium of a firm and industry under Perfect Competition. **[April 2011]**
4. What are the Characteristics of Perfect Competition? **[April 2008]**
5. Answer in brief:
   Explain the Features of Perfect Competition. **[April 2006, 2014, 2015, 2017, 2018]**

■■■

Unit **3**...

Pricing under Imperfect Market Conditions

Contents ...

Learning Objectives ...

- To understand the meaning of Imperfect Competition
- To learn about the features and Equilibrium in a Monopoly Market
- To elucidate Price Discrimination
- To know about the concept and features of Oligopoly and Duopoly
- To deliberate upon the comparison between Perfect and Imperfect Competition

3.1 MEANING OF IMPERECT COMPETITION

Most firms in real life lie somewhere between the two extremes of monopoly and perfect competition. The distance of real markets from the perfect market or monopoly market set two great economists - Joan Robinson of Cambridge University and Edward H. Chamberlin of Harvard University thinking on it. In 1933, Chamberlin published his book "The Theory of Monopolistic Competition" and in the same year, Joan Robinson published her book "The Economics of Imperfect Competition". They are considered to be the forerunners of the modern study of Imperfect Competition.

Their work was based on their study of the US market where few large firms dominated and distorted market conditions. They helped revolutionize economic theory, giving a new and more realistic description of markets.

In Imperfect Competition, there are many players but not as large as in perfect competition and each sells a differentiated product exercising some degree of market power, if not full. In real life, competition is rarely perfect. In the majority of cases, there is neither a single individual who controls the total supply, nor are there many sellers so that their individual shares are negligible in relation to the total supply of the market. Thus, the real situation is of imperfect competition where there is neither perfect competition nor absolute monopoly. This market situation is also known as Monopolistic Competition.

The Classical and Neo-Classical economists emphasized the competitive market situation as it would always increase material welfare. Imperfect competition as a market situation was given no importance. It was only after 1926, that the modern economists felt that absolute monopoly and perfect competition were unrealistic market situations.

Thus the terms Imperfect Competition or Monopolistic Competition are used to describe the market situations found in modern capitalist states, the basic features being a large number of firms selling differentiated products. Sometimes the term monopolistic competition is also referred to as Group Equilibrium.

3.2 MONOPOLY: MEANING AND TYPES

The term monopoly is derived from 'mono' (single) and 'poly' (selling). Thus 'monopoly' means a single control over the supply of output. Monopoly is that market form in which a single producer controls the entire supply of a commodity which has very few substitutes or no substitutes at all. Two points are to be noted with regard to the definition:

(i) There must be one producer or seller if there is to be a monopoly. That single producer may be an individual or a joint stock company or the state. As there is only one firm under monopoly, that single firm constitutes the whole industry. Therefore the distinction between firm and industry disappears under conditions of monopoly.

(ii) The commodity produced by the producer must have no close substitute if he is to be called a monopolist. This ensures that there is no rival for the commodity. Absence of close substitutes means there are no other firms producing a similar product or products varying slightly from that of the monopolist. For example, there are no close substitutes for electricity and water and since these are basic needs of the society, they are taken over by the state to prevent exploitation of consumers. This second condition of monopoly can be defined in terms of cross elasticity of demand (which shows a change in the demand for a commodity as a result of change in the price of another commodity). In case of pure monopoly the cross elasticity of demand between the product of the monopolist and the product of any other producer is zero. In case of imperfect monopoly the cross elasticity of demand is not zero but very low.

The above two conditions ensure that the monopolist can set the price of his product. Therefore the power to influence price is the very essence of monopoly. However, it must not be gathered that the monopolist is so powerful that he can dictate the price as well as the amount sold. The monopolist can do only one thing at a time; either he can fix the price leaving the amount sold upon the consumers, or he can fix the quantity he wants to produce and sell and leave the price to be determined by the demand of the consumers.

Features of Monopoly:

1. A monopolist is a single producer or seller. Therefore firm and industry are identical.
2. There are no close substitutes to what the monopolist produces or sells. Therefore buyers have no choice, either to buy the commodity or go without it.
3. A monopolist is a 'price maker'. If he is a discriminating monopolist, he can vary the price from buyer to buyer.
4. A monopolist can maintain his position as the sole producer or seller of a product only when certain circumstances keep the rivals or competitors away from his line of production. The barriers to entry may be legal, technological, and financial barriers.
5. In monopoly the firm is also the industry. Therefore the firm faces a downward sloping demand curve for its product implying that more output can be sold only at a lower price.
6. Monopoly is a complete negation of competition.

Types of Monopoly:

1. **Pure Monopoly and Imperfect Monopoly:**
   - **Pure Monopoly** means a single firm which controls the supply of a commodity which has no substitutes. It possesses absolute monopoly power. Such a monopoly is rare.
   - **Imperfect Monopoly** means a limited degree of monopoly. It refers to a single firm which produces a commodity having no close substitutes. The degree of monopoly is less than perfect in this case and it relates to the availability of a close substitute. In practice, there are many cases of such imperfect monopoly. Imperfect monopoly does not rule out the possibility of competition. It implies a threat of competition from the rivals producing remote substitutes. Hence imperfect monopoly lacks absolute monopoly power in deciding price and output policy.
2. **Legal, Natural, Technological and Joint Monopolies:**

   On the basis of sources of deriving monopoly power, monopolies may be classified as:
   - **Legal monopolies** emerge on account of legal provisions like patents, trademarks, copyrights etc. The law forbids the potential competitors to imitate the design and form of products registered under the given brand names, patents or trademarks.
   - **Natural advantages** like good location, old-age establishment, involvement of huge investment, business reputation etc confer **natural monopolies** on many firms.
   - **Technological expertise,** economies of large scale and efficiency of superior capital use and the process of mechanization etc., confer technological monopolies to big firms.
   - **Through business combinations** like trusts, cartels, syndicates etc., some firms may unite in a group and acquire **joint monopolies** in the market.
3. **Simple Monopoly and Discriminating Monopoly:**
   - **A simple monopoly** firm charges a uniform price for its product to all the buyers. It operates in a single market.
   - **A discriminating monopoly** firm charges different prices for the same product to different buyers. It operates in more than one market.

4. **Private Monopoly and Public or Social Monopoly:**

   Considering the nature of ownership, monopolies may be grouped into:

   - **Private monopolies:** when an individual or a private body controls a monopoly firm, it is regarded as a private monopoly.
   - **Public or Social Monopoly:** when production is solely owned, controlled and operated by the state, it is regarded as a social or public monopoly. Public monopolies are confined to nationalized industries.

Causes of Monopoly:

1. A firm may own or control the entire supply of a raw material required in the production of a commodity, or the firm may possess some unique managerial talent.
2. A firm may own a patent for the exclusive right to produce a commodity or to use a particular production process.
3. Economies of scale may operate (i.e. the long run average cost curve may fall) over a sufficiently large range of outputs so as to leave a single firm supplying the entire market. Such a firm is called a **natural monopoly.** Examples of natural monopolies are electricity, water and gas. To have more than one firm supplying electricity, water and gas services in a given market would lead to overlapping distribution systems and much higher per unit costs.
4. A firm may become a monopolist because it is awarded a market franchise, licensed by a Government agency. In exchange for this right, the firm agrees to allow the Government to regulate certain aspects of its operations, like standards of competency.

Determination of output under Monopoly

Two important points about the equilibrium position of a monopolist is to be noted:

(i) The monopolist is in equilibrium in the elastic segment of his demand curve (i.e. where elasticity of demand, is greater than one). This can be illustrated as follows:

In the (Fig. 3.1) as long as MR > O, TR is rising. When MR = 0 at point Q the TR is maximum, and when MR < O the TR declines. When MR > 0 or TR is raising the elasticity of demand is greater than one. When MR = 0 or TR is maximum, elasticity of demand is equal to one. When MR < O or TR declines, the elasticity of demand is less than one.

The monopolist will always produce and sell a level of output which corresponds to the elastic segment of his downward sloping demand curve. As long as the elasticity of demand (AR curve) is greater than one, the MR though declining is +ve i.e. there is an increase in TR.

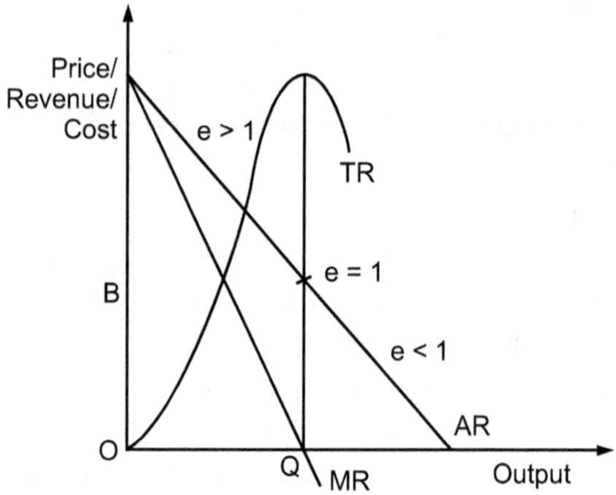

Fig. 3.1

Reduction of price at a point where the elasticity of demand is greater than one leads to an increase in sales more than proportionate to the fall in price. Where elasticity of demand is equal to one (unity) MR = 0. i.e. there is no change in TR with a fall in price. Where elasticity of demand is less than one, MR is −ve i.e. there is a fall in TR with a decrease in price.

The equilibrium output under any market structure is determined at the point where MC = MR and MC cuts MR curve from below. When **MR is -ve** at those levels of output where elasticity of demand is less than one, the MC and MR curve cannot be equal. This is because MC can never be negative. Therefore the monopolist cannot be in equilibrium at those output levels where elasticity of demand is less than one.

There are some cases where cost of production is **zero** or is not relevant to the pricing decision. For example, in case of mineral springs, cost of production is zero. Further, in the very short run, if a good is already on hand in excessive amount, cost of production is not relevant for fixing price. However these situations are rare.

When **MR is positive,** the elasticity of demand (AR) is greater than one. The monopolist will fix his output at a point where

MC = MR and MC cuts MR from below. This is now possible because with every addition in output, MC rises therefore it is positive.

Hence, it can be concluded that the equilibrium of the monopolist will always lie at that level of output where the elasticity of demand for his product is greater than one, provided that his costs are positive, i.e. he will not produce output beyond OQ (refer Fig. 3.1.)

(ii) Monopoly equilibrium output is determined at the falling path of the AC curve, which means that the monopolist restricts output before producing it at the optimum level of minimum AC in order to maximise his profit. This is clear in Fig. 3.2.

Monopoly Equilibrium in the Short Run

Since a single firm constitutes the whole industry under monopoly there is no need for a separate analysis of the equilibrium of the firm and industry. A monopoly firm would attain equilibrium when MR = rising MC. In such a case, a monopoly firm can

(i) Earn super normal profits or
(ii) Normal profit or
(iii) Even incur losses

(i) Case of Super Normal Profits (AR > AC)

A monopolist earns SNP when his AR > AC. A monopolist earning SNP in the short run continues to do so even in the long run because the monopolist creates barriers of entry i.e. preventing other firms from entering into the industry.

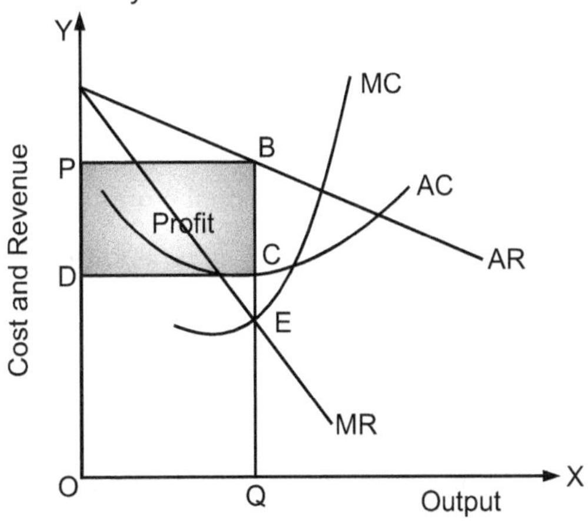

Fig. 3.2: Case of Super Normal Profits (SNP)

In the above Fig. 3.2, the equilibrium output is at output level OQ where MR = rising MC. The price at which the output is sold is OP. The AC being lower than the AR the monopolist makes SNP to the extent of BC per unit of output and DPBC for output OQ. It may be noted that the equilibrium output of a monopoly firm is determined at the falling part of AC. This output is less than optimum.

(ii) Normal Profits: (AR = AC)

It is possible that a monopolist faces a situation where AR = AC. This arises specially in the case of state produced goods where the price at which the output sold is exactly equal to cost and no price over and above the cost of production is charged. This is to ensure the supply of basic goods to the consumers at a reasonable rate.

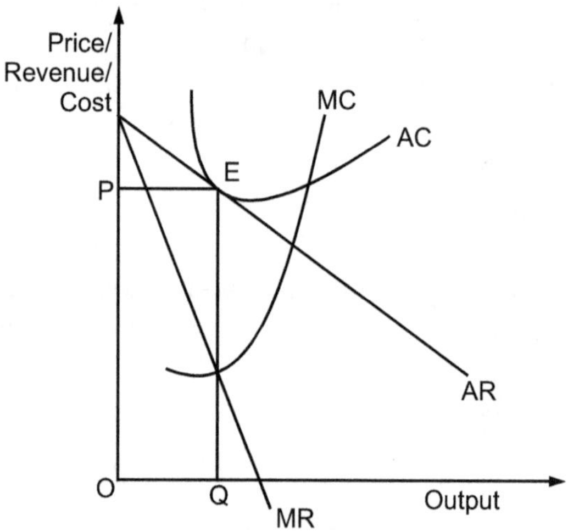

Fig. 3.3: Case of Normal Profits

In the above Fig. 3.3, AR = AC i.e. EQ = EQ and the output OQ is sold at price OP.

(iii) Case of Losses (AR < AC):

It is possible that an inefficient monopolist incurs losses in the short run. However, he does not continue to do so in the long run.

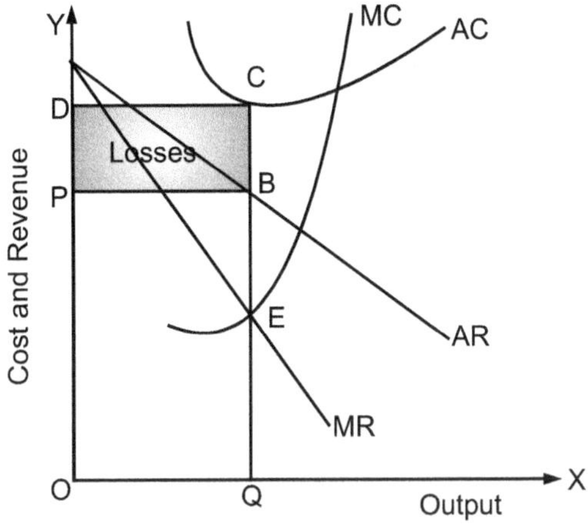

Fig. 3.4: Case of Losses

In the above Fig. 3.4, AR < AC. Hence the monopolist incurs a loss of CB per unit of output and PDCB for output OQ.

Monopoly Equilibrium in the Long Run:

A monopoly firm attains long run equilibrium when LMR = LMC and LMC cuts LMR from below. In the long run the monopoly firms enjoys:

(i) SNP or

(ii) Normal profits.

If there are losses in the short run period and if they continue even in the long run, the monopoly firm will close down or change the size of its plant.

(i) Case of SNP (LAR > LAC):

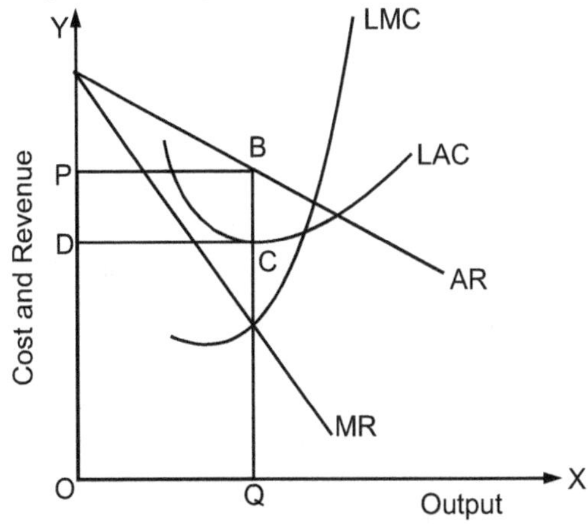

Fig. 3.5: Case of SNP

In the above Fig. 3.5, the monopolist earns SNP of BC per unit of output and DPBC for output OQ. He earns SNP in the long run because the entry of new firms is closed.

(ii) Case of Normal Profits (LAR = LAC):

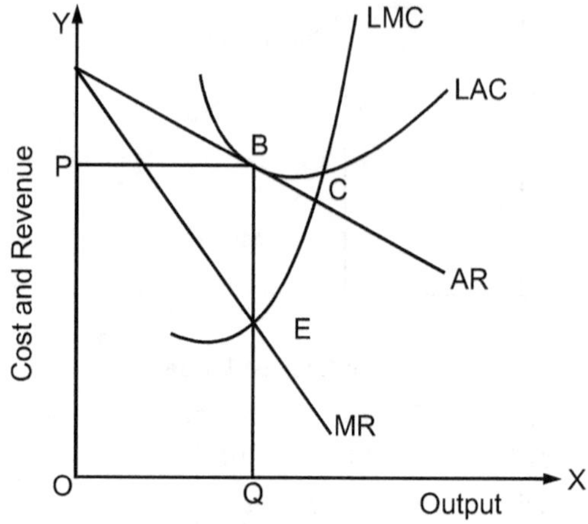

Fig. 3.6: Case of Normal Profits

In the above Fig. 3.6, the monopolist earns normal profits as LAR = LAC at point B. The output OQ is sold at price OP.

Comparison between Perfect Competition and Monopoly

1. Under perfect competition, the demand curve or the AR curve faced by an individual firm is perfectly elastic and is a horizontal straight line parallel to the X-axis. Therefore MR = AR at all levels of output and hence MR coincides with the AR curve. Unlike this, under monopoly, the demand on AR curve faced by the firm falls downwards from left to right. Therefore MR is less than AR at all levels of output and the MR lies below the AR curves. (Refer Fig. 3.1).

2. Both under perfect competition and monopoly the firm is in equilibrium at that level of output where MR = rising MC. But in perfect competition since MR = AR or price, MC when equal to MR in equilibrium condition is also equal to price or AR. This is not true in case of monopoly. Since under monopoly MR is always less than AR or price, in equilibrium therefore MC will be equal to MR but less than AR or price. Hence under perfect competition MC = MR = AR (price) under monopoly it will be MC = MR < AR (price). (Refer Fig. 3.2)

Thus in perfectly competitive equilibrium the price charged by the firm equals its marginal cost, under monopoly the price set is above the marginal cost. In fact, the difference between marginal cost and price is said to measure the degree of monopoly power.

3. Basically the difference between a competitive firm and a firm under monopoly arises from the fact that under perfect competition, the supply of output comes from the innumerable number of sellers each selling a small quantity. While in monopoly, there is only one firm controlling the entire supply of the product. Perfect competition implies the existence of a large number of buyers and sellers all competing with each other. Monopoly refers to the existence of a single firm in the industry producing a particular commodity or service. The monopolist can either charge a uniform price or different prices from different buyers. Under perfect competition the price is fixed by the market and the producer cannot exercise any control over it.
4. In perfect competition a firm is in the long run equilibrium at the minimum point of the LAC curve. In monopoly the firm is in equilibrium at the point where AC is still declining and has not reached the minimum. The chief reason for this limitation of output is that, as output is increased MR drops below this, thus lowering AR, whereas MC is likely to increase. Under perfect competition, it pays the firm to expand production so long as the AC is falling, because under perfect competition AR and MR both stay high for a large output as for small output. (Refer Fig. 3.5 or Fig. 3.6)
5. Another difference between the monopoly equilibrium and perfectly competitive equilibrium is that, while under perfect competition, in the long run, a firm can earn only normal profits; under monopoly the firm can earn SNP even in the long run. If a perfectly competitive firm earns SNP in the short run, they are competed away in the long run by the entry of new firms in the industry. But in case of monopoly, there are sufficient barriers to the entry of new firms in the industry. Therefore new firms cannot enter the industry in the long run to compete away the monopoly profits. (Fig. 3.5). But it must not be thought that monopoly always guarantees SNPs. If the demand and cost situation is not favourable (refer Fig. 3.4), the monopolist may suffer short run losses. But it must earn normal profits or more in the long run otherwise it will leave its business.

6. Under monopoly the price set is higher and output smaller than under perfect competition, given the same cost revenue situation. This is so because the monopolist restricts output to raise price. This can be illustrated as follows:

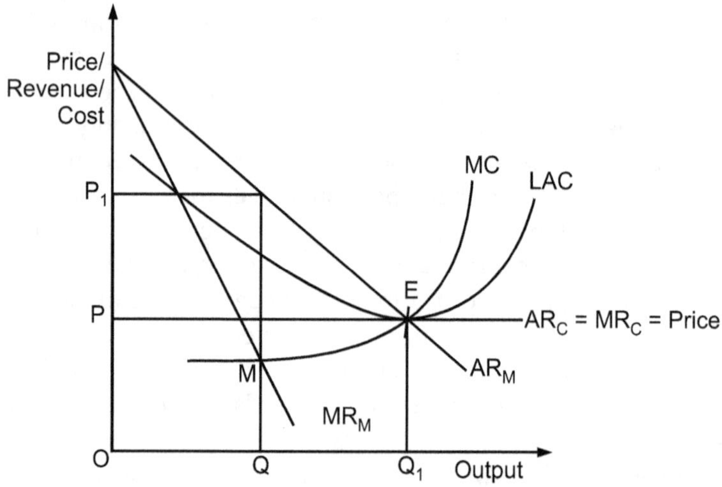

Fig. 3.7

In the above figure (Fig. 3.7), in perfect competition the MC cuts MR curve from below at point E and output is OQ. (Since AR = MR = price.) Under monopoly the AR and MR curves are downward sloping. The MC curve cuts MR (from below) of monopoly at point M i.e. output OQ. Since AR is above the MR curve the output OQ is sold at price OP. Therefore it can be concluded that the output under perfect competition (OQ_1) is greater than the output under monopoly (OQ) and the price under perfect competition (OP) is less than the price under monopoly (OP_1), gives the same cost revenue situation.

7. Economic welfare of the community would be maximised when there is the most efficient allocation of resources for production and consumption. Competitive firms maximise the welfare of the consumers and is therefore in the interest of the society at large. On the other hand a monopolist produces output at less than optimum size i.e. at a higher AC i.e. there is unutilized capacity of the plant and resources. Further the monopoly price is higher than perfect competitive price and sometimes a monopolist also adopts the policy of price discrimination in order to maximise profits. All this is against the interest of the consumers.

Discriminating Monopoly or Price Discrimination

Price discrimination refers to a situation where a monopolist charges different prices from different customers for the same commodity. A monopolist who adopts the policy of price discrimination is known as 'discriminating monopoly'. In the words of Joan Robinson "the act of selling the same article, produced under single control at different prices to different buyers is known as price discrimination." Price discrimination cannot be practised under conditions of perfect competition. The assumptions of perfect competition like large number of buyers and sellers of a homogeneous commodity are such that only one price prevails in the market. Therefore there is no scope for price discrimination. Discrimination between buyers is possible only under conditions of monopoly.

Forms of Price Discriminations

1. **Personal discrimination:** This occurs when different prices are charged from different persons buying the same commodity. This is more common in the case of personal services, which may be based on the income of the customers. For example, doctors, lawyers, teachers can charge different fees from different customers.
2. **Age discrimination:** This is price discrimination on the basis of age of buyers. For example in buses and trains, the fares are different for adults and children.
3. **Locational or territorial or geographical or simply place discrimination:** Here different prices are charged in different markets located in different places. For example a firm may discriminate between domestic market (lower price) and export markets (higher price).
4. **Size discrimination:** Different prices are charged for different sizes or different quantities of the same product. For example 200 gm toothpaste may cost relatively less than 100 gm toothpaste.
5. **Quality variation discrimination:** Different prices may be charged for the same product on the basis of qualitative differences. For example a student edition of a book costs less than the original edition of the same book.
6. **Use discrimination:** Different prices are charged for the same product for different uses. For example, electricity charges are

lower for industrial uses compared to domestic consumption. Similarly, railways charge less freight rates for certain goods like coal, food grains etc.

7. **Time discrimination:** Under time discrimination, the price of the same product differs at different times. Here the examples are STD and telegram charges. The day time and night time charges for them are different. On account of maximum idle capacity during night, dialing rates are minimum at night. This helps in achieving optimum utilisation of capacity.

Degrees of Price Discrimination

According to P.C. Pigou, there are three degrees of price discrimination:

1. **First degree price discrimination:** This occurs when a monopolist charges a different price against different uses of a commodity in such a way that there is no consumer's surplus left with the buyers. (Consumer's surplus is defined as the difference between what a consumer actually pays for a product and what he would be willing to pay for it rather than go without it). This is also referred to as Perfect Discrimination. It is possible only when buyers are few so that each one can be dealt with individually and the monopolist fully knows what maximum they would pay for each unit of his product.
2. **Second degree price discrimination:** Under this category a monopolist charges different prices for the same commodity. He allows some consumers surplus which may be done to satisfy the consumers and to shelter the market from potential rivals. The monopolist divides the market into different groups and from each group a different price is charged. This sort of price discrimination is feasible when the total market for the product is very wide, with a large number of buyers having different tastes, different incomes, and different conditions, so that sub-divisions of the market or groups of buyers can be easily made.
3. **Third degree price discrimination:** This is the most common kind of price discrimination. In this the seller charges two different prices in two different markets, sub- markets or groups situated at different places. The most important condition for this kind of price discrimination is that the elasticity of demand in the two markets must be different. The price will be high in the market with less elastic demand and the price will be low in the market with high elastic demand.

When is price discrimination possible?

Price discrimination is possible in the following conditions:

1. **Segmentation of the Market:** If total market can be divided into sub-markets and if one sub-market has no connection with the others and if consumers have no inclination to move from a high-priced market to a low-priced market due to ignorance or laziness, then price discrimination is possible.
2. **Apparent product differentiation:** The same good is generally converted into different varieties by providing different packings, different names or labels in order to convince the buyer that certain varieties are superior to others. In this way, the producers are able to sell the so-called superior varieties to the rich people at higher prices and the so-called inferior varieties to the poor people.
3. **Non transferable characteristics of goods:** The nature of the commodity or service may be such that there is no possibility of transfer from one market to another. For example the sale of direct personal services, like that of a surgeon or lawyer. The surgeons usually charge different fees from the rich and the poor for the same kind of operation. This is possible since the service has to be delivered personally by the surgeon and therefore it cannot be transferred.
4. **Prevention of resale or re-exchange of goods:** Goods should not be re-exchangeable between buyers of a low-priced market and a high priced market due to geographical distance, high cost of transport etc.
5. **Buyer's prejudices or illusions:** When buyers irrationally feel that high priced goods are better in quality, the monopolist can resort to price discrimination.
6. **Sometimes there may be legal sanctions for price discrimination:** When, in some cases, price discrimination is legally sanctioned, the transfer of use of the product is legally prohibited in order to make it effective. For instance, if electricity, for domestic purposes is used for commercial purposes, the customer is liable to be penalized.

When is Price Discrimination Profitable?

Price discrimination is profitable only if elasticity of demand in one market is different from the elasticity of demand in the other. Therefore the monopolist will discriminate prices between two markets only when he finds that the elasticity of demand for his product is different in the two sub-markets.

When elasticities of demand in both the markets are different, the monopolist can charge a high price where demand is more inelastic and he charges a low price and allows the sales to increase where the demand is more elastic. Reduction in supply to the market where demand is inelastic results in increasing TR. When elasticity of demand is less than 1, a fall in price results in contraction of TR and a rise in price leads to an expansion of TR. On the contrary, where elasticity of demand is greater than 1, a fall in price leads to an increase in TR. Therefore it will be profitable for the monopolist to reduce his supply in the market where demand is inelastic so that the price can rise. The same supply can be diverted to the other market where demand is elastic. Thus it will result in a fall in the price and an increase in the TR. This policy will cause an increase in TR in both the markets. The act of diverting supply from one market to the other will continue until the MRs in both the markets is equal.

Equilibrium of a Discriminating Monopolist

The price discriminating monopolist has to decide:

(i) The total output to be produced,

(ii) How much of the total output should be sold in each market so that profits are maximum.

(iii) The prices to be charged in different markets.

Let us assume that the monopolist wishes to sell his output in two separate markets. The demand for the product in Market 1 is relatively inelastic and that in Market 2 is relatively elastic.

Conditions for Equilibrium:

(i) $\Sigma MR = MC$ ($\Sigma MR = MR_1 + MR_2$) and

(ii) MC cuts Σ MR from below.

(iii) $MR_1 = MR_2$.

The equilibrium of a discriminating monopolist can be illustrated as follows:

In the above diagram (Fig. 3.8) ΣMR represents the aggregate MR curve. At point E, MC curve cuts ΣMR from below. Therefore it is the profit maximising equilibrium condition and OQ is the equilibrium output.

The monopolist now distributes this OQ output in such a way that $MR_1 = MR_2$. To determine this, a horizontal line AE parallel to the X-axis is drawn. The line crosses the MR_1 curve at point 'a' and MR_2 curve at point 'b'.

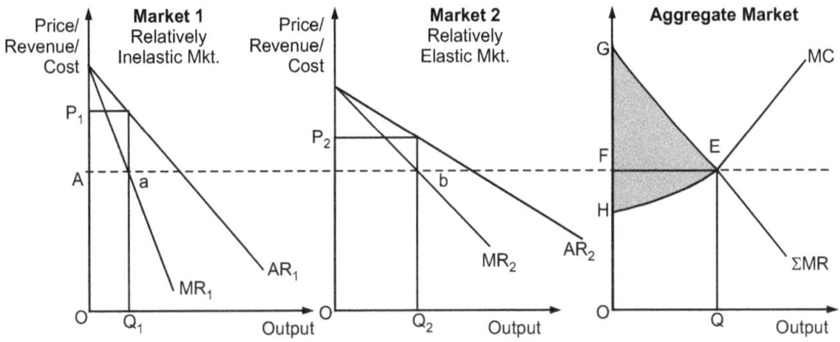

Fig. 3.8: Equilibrium of a Discriminating Monopolist

Correspondingly OQ_1 and OQ_2 quantities of output are determined for allocation in the two markets respectively.

OQ_1 is allocated to Market 1 and sold at price OP_1.

OQ_2 is sold in Market 2 at price OP_2.

$$OQ_1 + OQ_2 = OQ$$

$$\Sigma MR = MR_1 = MR_2 \ (EQ = aQ_1 = bQ_2).$$

$$\text{Profit} = TR - TC$$

$$= OGEQ - OHEQ$$

Therefore **Profit = HGE.**

It can be observed that

$OQ_1 < OQ_2$ but

$OP_1 > OP_2$

i.e. where demand is relatively inelastic, price charged is high and amount supplied is less. Where demand is relatively elastic, a large quantity is supplied and the price charged is low.

3.3 MONOPOLISTIC COMPETITION

Features: Both perfect competition and perfect or pure monopoly are theoretical extremes and uncommon in reality. What exists in reality is imperfect competition. Monopolistic competition is one form of imperfect competition. The term monopolistic competition was first used by Prof. E. H. Chamberlin in his book "The Theory of Monopolistic Competition" published in 1933 and developed by Mrs Joan Robinson in her book "Economics of Imperfect Competition."

Monopolistic competition refers to a market situation in which there are a large number of sellers each having some degree of monopoly power and selling products which are similar (but not identical) or differentiated and are close substitutes of one another. It is a blend of competition and monopoly. It is found in many fields: soaps, toothpastes, shampoos, cosmetics, soft drinks, electrical appliances, barber's saloons, chemist shops, cloth stores etc.

Following are some of the characteristic features of monopolistic competition:

1. **Large number of sellers:** Under monopolistic competition there are **many firms,** each selling closely related but not identical products. An individual firm has relatively small part of the total market so that each has a very limited control over the price of the product. Again, the presence of relatively large number of firms ensures that collusion by them to restrict output to raise price is most unlikely. With a large number of firms there is no mutual interdependence i.e. each firm determines its price-output policies without considering the possible reactions of rival firms. Once an equilibrium price is set in a particular line of production, the new entrant has to follow it and can change the price only in the vicinity of that range. But a monopolistically competitive firm is not a price-taker and can adopt an independent **price and production policy.**
2. **Freedom of entry and exit of firms:** As in perfect competition, in monopolistic competition too, there is freedom of entry and exit in the long run i.e. there are no barriers to entry and firms can enter or quit freely.
3. **Product differentiation:** The product is not homogeneous. Each product is branded and identified and distinguished from the rest. There may be differences in packing, trademark and salesmanship. Therefore buyer's preferences are created and buyers are induced to choose a particular seller and stick to him. Product differentiation creates brand loyalty of the consumers and the products are commonly known by brand names or trademarks. This is one of the most distinguishing features of monopolistic competition.
4. **Selling costs or Sales Promotion:** This is an important feature of monopolistic competition. The outlays incurred on

advertisements, publicity, salesmanship and other forms of sales promotion are called selling costs. Under perfect competition there is no need for selling costs because goods are homogeneous. Since products are differentiated under monopolistic competition, there is need for selling costs. Selling costs are incurred with the objective of shifting the demand curve for the product (and capturing a wider market). The demand curve for a monopolistic competitive firm is downward sloping, but relatively elastic compared to a monopoly firm. This is because of a large number of competitors selling similar products as close substitutes. Further, larger the number of firms larger the elasticity of demand.

5. **The concept of Group:** Since each firm produces a somewhat different product under monopolistic competition, we cannot define the industry (which refers to the producers of an **identical** product). Chamberlin, who introduced the theory of monopolistic competition sought to overcome this difficulty by lumping all the **sellers** of similar products into a **product group.**

6. **Two types of competition:** There are two types of competition under monopolistic competition-

    (a) Price competition: where firms compete with each other on the basis of price variation;

    (b) Non-price competition: where firms also compete with each other by varying their products and selling costs.

Short run equilibrium of a Firm under Monopolistic Competition

A firm is in equilibrium when it maximises its profits i.e. where MR = rising MC. Under monopolistic competition the demand curve (AR) is downward sloping and more elastic compared to a monopoly firm. The degree of elasticity of the AR curve depends on -

(i) Number of firms in the group: larger the number of firms (or more severe the competition), the greater the elasticity of demand. If the number of firms is small, demand tends to be relatively less elastic.

(ii) Extent of product differentiation: If product differentiation is relatively weak, demand tends to be elastic. If product differentiation is prominently significant then demand tends to be less elastic.

1. Case of SNP (AR > SAC):

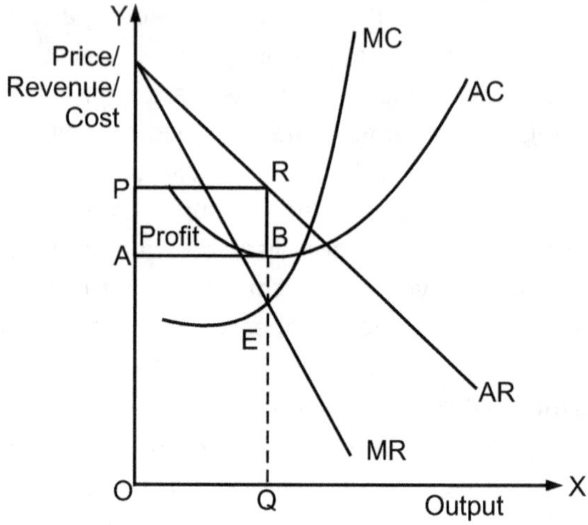

Fig. 3.9: Case of SNP

In the above Fig. 3.9, RQ is the AR and BQ is the AC. Therefore RB is SNP per unit of output. Total SNP is APRB for output level OQ.

2. Case of Losses (AR < SAC):

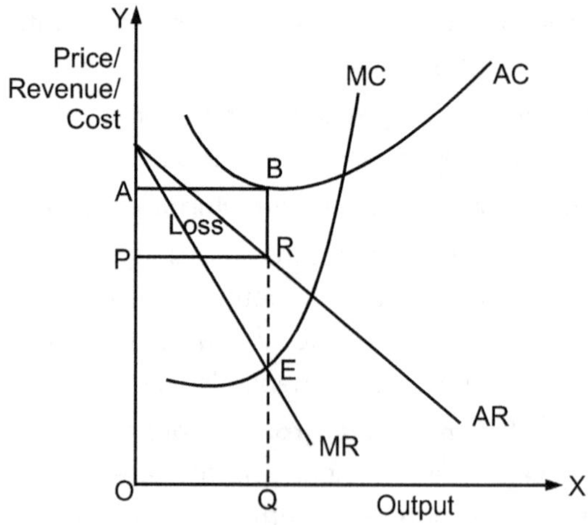

Fig. 3.10: Case of Losses

In the above Fig. 3.10, the demand and cost situations are less favourable. Hence the firm incurs loss of BR per unit of output and a total loss of ABRP for output level OQ.

1. Case of Normal Profits (AR=AC):

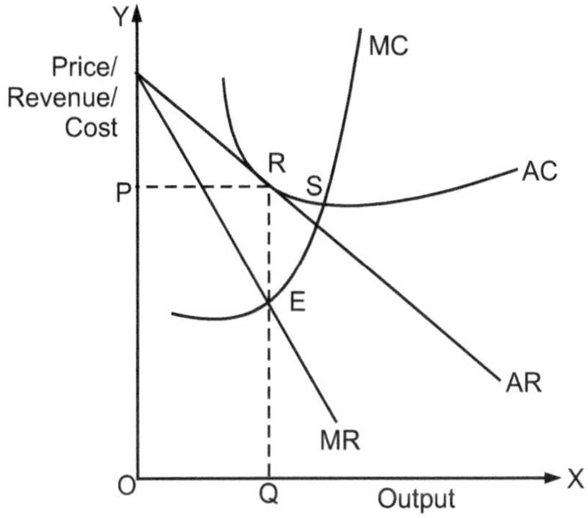

Fig. 3.11: Case of Normal Profits

In the above Fig. 3.11, the cost and revenue conditions are such that the firm under monopolistic competition earns normal profits where AR = AC i.e. at output level OQ, RQ = RQ.

Thus in the short run, a monopolistically competitive firm may either realise SNP or suffer losses or earn normal profits.

Long run Equilibrium of a Firm under Monopolistic Competition

We have seen that the firms under monopolistic competition can earn SNPs in the short run. But in the long run, such profits disappear. This is because with the entry of new firms in the industry supply will increase, prices will fall and the SNP will be competed away and the firms will be earning only normal profits. If, in a short run, firms are realising losses, then in the long run, some firms will leave the industry so that the remaining firms will be earning normal profits. Further in the long run equilibrium AR curve will be more elastic (i.e. flatter) since large number of substitutes will be available in the long run. Thus there is equilibrium in the long run when MC = MR = AR = AC.

This can be illustrated as follows:

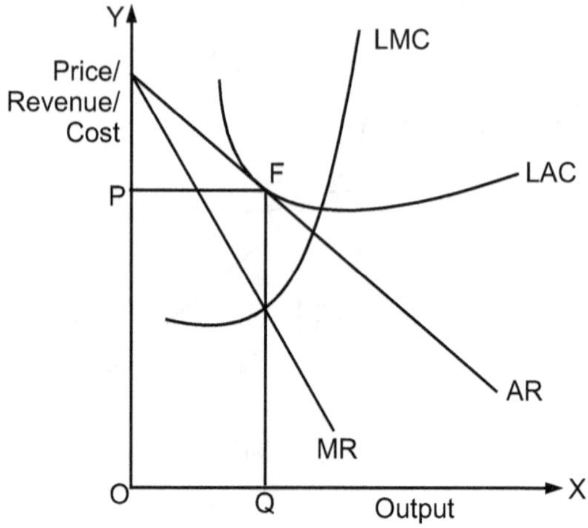

Fig. 3.12

In the above diagram (Fig. 3.12) the firm is in equilibrium at output OQ and price OP. In this case AR = LAC. Hence there is **normal profit.**

Non-Price Competition

1. Product Differentiation

A general class of product is differentiated if a basis exists for preferring goods of one seller to those of another. Such a basis for preference may be real or fancied, but it will cause differentiation of the product. When such differentiation of the product exists, even if it is slight, buyers will be paired with sellers not in a random fashion (as in perfect competition) but according to their preferences. There are two bases of product differentiation.

1. Differentiation may be based upon certain characteristics of the product itself such as exclusive patented features, trademarks and trade names, peculiarities of packages or wrappers if any or difference in quality, design, colour or style. Real qualitative differences like those of materials used, design and workmanship are no doubt important means of differentiating products. But imaginary differences created through advertising, the use of attractive packets, the use of trademarks and brand names are more usual methods by which products are differentiated, even if physically they are identical or almost so.
2. Differentiation may be based upon the conditions surrounding the sale of the product. This means that product is differentiated

if the services rendered in the process of selling the product by one seller or firm are not identical with those rendered by any other seller or firm. The conditions surrounding the sale of the product include the convenience of the seller's location, the general tone or character of his establishment, his way of doing business, his reputation for fair dealing, courtesy, efficiency and all others which attach his customers either to himself or those employed by him.

Product differentiation may range from strong to weak but it influences the consumers' psychology and preference or choice. Product differentiation, whether real or fancied, identifies the seller and confers on him a degree of monopoly power which he can exploit well to capture a segment of the market.

Product differentiation has two aspects:

(i) Product differentiation at a **point of time** - this aims at identifying the product of the seller from the product of rivals.

(ii) Product development or quality variation over a period of time - over a **long period of time,** when sellers resort to product competition, they adopt quality variation or improvement in the product. The product is adjusted more sensitively to the tastes and preferences of consumers, which ensures their strong patronage. By resorting to product improvement and giving a new brand name to it, the producer hopes to have a more inelastic demand for his product and therefore the demand curve shifts to the right but is more inelastic. Therefore he can charge a higher price than what was charged for the old variety, without losing patronage. For example: TV manufacturers making technical improvements in their sets, new editions of text books.

Therefore product differentiation is a facet of **non-price competition** in a monopolistic group. This is illustrated as follows:

In the Fig. 3.13, with improved varieties L, M, N of the product the firm faces more and more inelastic demand as well as a demand curve further up to the right such as D_1D_1, D_2D_2 and D_3D_3. The producer can charge a higher price than before without experiencing any market contraction in the sale of his product or if he continues to charge the same price, he finds an increase in the demand for his product.

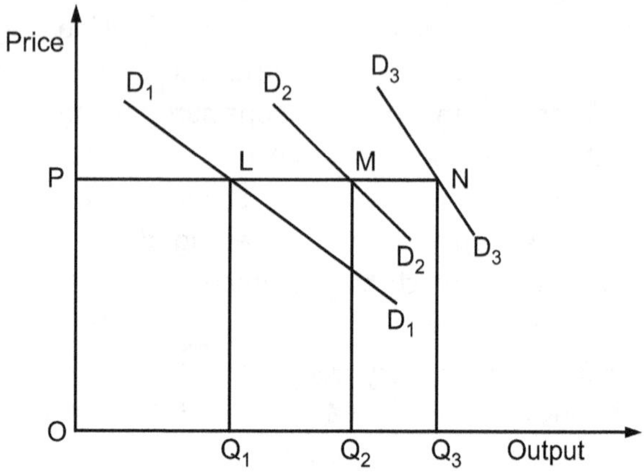

Fig. 3.13

2. Selling Costs:

The expenditure incurred by a firm on advertising and sales promotion of its product is known as selling costs. According to Chamberlin, selling costs include "advertising in its many forms, salaries of salesmen and the expenses of sales departments and sales agencies, window displays and displays and demonstrations of all kinds."

There are two kinds of advertising:

(a) Promotional or informative advertising.

(b) Manipulative or competitive or persuasive advertising.

(a) Promotional or informative advertising: According to Chamberlin, ignorance of the products on the part of the consumer is an important reason for advertising. Buyers may lack information as regards the different sellers in a given line of product and the differences in the quality of their products. Therefore a seller may resort to "informative advertising" i.e. he may describe the quality and price of his product and thereby try to influence the shape and location of the demand curve. By spreading information about the product through advertising, the firm's demand curve shifts to the right and becomes less elastic.

(b) Manipulative/Competitive/Persuasive advertising: Each firm under monopolistic competition tries to convince the buyers that its product is better than those of others in the group. It seeks to increase the demand for its product by increasing the amount of advertisement expenditure and through it, persuading the buyers that its brand of the product is of superior quality than others. Thus, this is competitive advertising, which is aimed at attracting the customers to their product and weaning them away from the closely related products of the rivals. Thus the fundamental aim of all competitive advertising is to attract the customer's attention and to imprint the name of a particular product on his mind and to increase the sales of one firm at the expense of others. Such competitive advertising by a firm often proves to be successful in its objective of increasing the demand for a particular brand of the product and as a result of advertisement, demand curve facing an individual firm shifts to the right. This implies that at a given price, greater quantity of the product can be sold.

Distinction between Selling Costs and Production Costs

1. According to Chamberlin, production costs include all those expenses which are incurred to manufacture and provide a product to the consumer to meet his given demand or want; while selling costs are those which are incurred to change, alter or create the demand for a product. Production costs include manufacturing costs, transportation costs and cost of handling, storing and delivering a product to the consumers. Selling costs include all outlays made in order to secure a demand or market for the market.
2. Production costs create utilities in order that demands may be satisfied. Selling costs create and shift the demand themselves. I.e. of all the costs incurred in the manufacture and sale of a given product those which alter the demand curve for it are selling costs and those which do not are production costs.
3. According to Chamberlin, those costs which are "made to adapt the product to the demand are costs of production (production costs); those made to adapt the demand to the product are costs of selling (selling costs)".
4. When production cost increases, the supply of the product increases. When selling cost increases, the demand for the product increases.

In practice, production costs and selling costs are intermixed and it is difficult to separate one from the other. However, in determining the price, it is obvious that production costs and selling costs must be covered by the firm if it is to remain in business.

Average Selling Cost (ASC) and Marginal Selling Cost (MSC):

ASC = TSC/Q where

TSC = Total Selling Cost

Q = Output

MSC = $TSC_n - TSC_{n-1}$

The ASC curve is U shaped and the MSC passes through its minimum as follows:

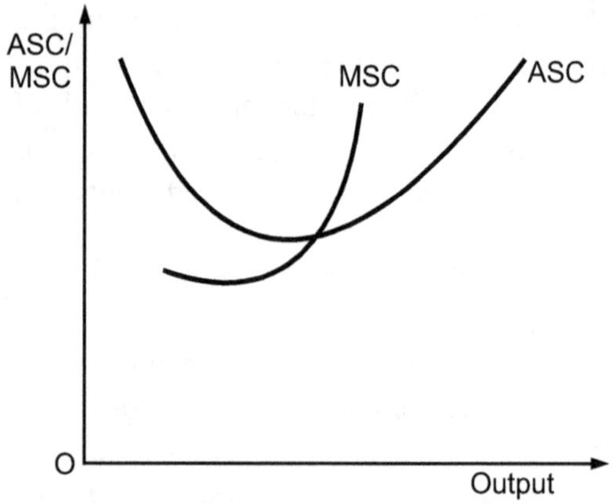

Fig. 3.14: The ASC and the MSC Curves

Combined Costs: The combined cost is the summation of production cost and selling cost.

CAC = APC + ASC

CAC = Combined average cost

APC = Average production cost

ASC = Average selling cost

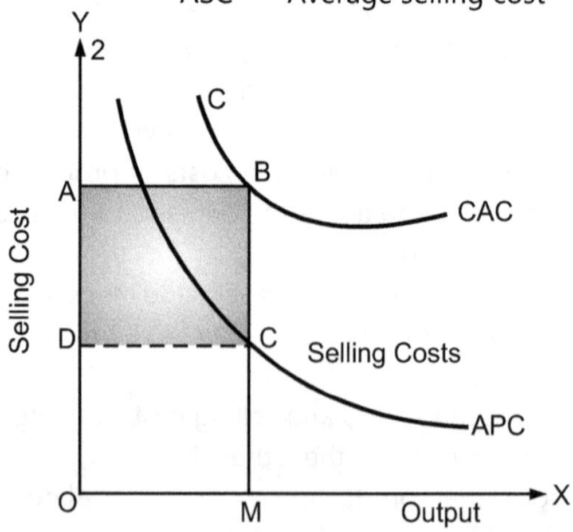

Fig. 3.15

In the above Fig. 3.15, the vertical distance between CAC and APC is ASC. For instance, for OM level of output, CM is the average production cost and BM the average combined cost. Thus BC is the average selling cost. At OM level of output, total production cost is OMCD and the total combined cost is OMBA. Therefore, ABCD measures the total selling costs.

Equilibrium of a firm incurring Advertising Expenses

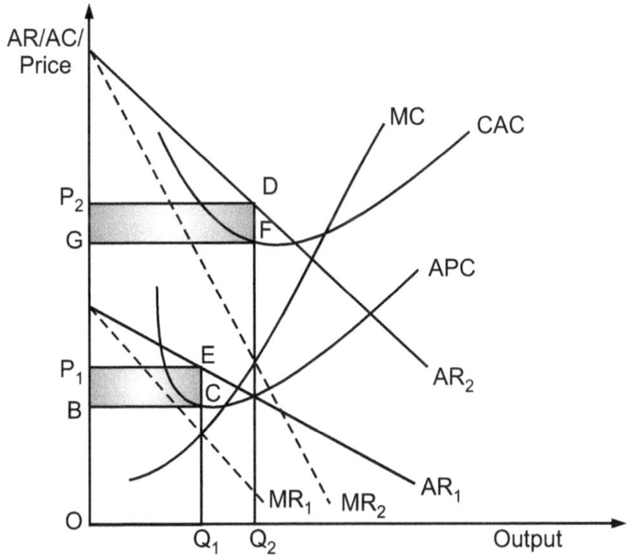

Fig. 3.16

In the above Fig. 3.16, let AR_1 be the demand curve or AR curve for the product and APC is the average production cost curve which does not include any selling or advertising cost. Let equilibrium output be OQ_1 (where MC cuts MR_1 from below) and price determined be OP_1. The profit earned is BP_1EC.

Suppose the firm decides to undertake advertisement expenses. This advertisement expenditure will not only increase demand by shifting the AR curve to the right to AR_2 and making it more inelastic compared to AR_1 but will also add to costs. Therefore the new combined AC curve (includes advertising cost or selling cost) is CAC. Now equilibrium output is OQ_2 and price charged is OP_2 and the profits have increased to GP_2DF.

Excess Capacity under Monopolistic Competition

Theories of Chamberlin's monopolistic competition and Joan Robinson's imperfect competition have revealed that a firm under monopolistic competition or imperfect competition in the long-run equilibrium produces an output which is less than socially optimum or ideal output. This means that firms operate at the point on the falling portion of LAC curve i.e. they do not produce the level of output at which LAC is minimum. This is illustrated as follows:

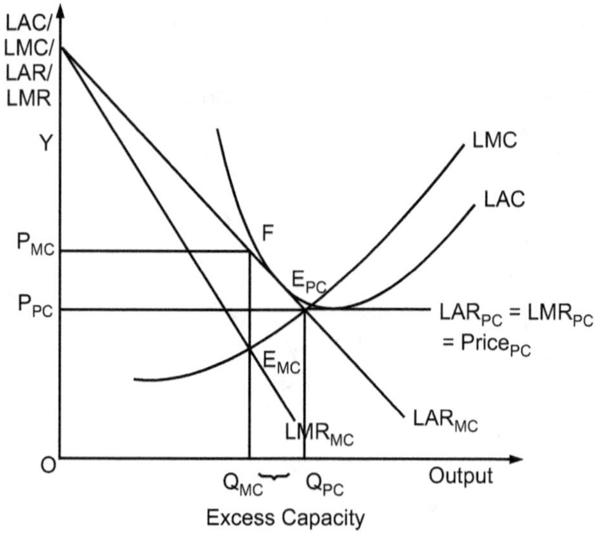

Fig. 3.17

In the above Fig. 3.17, the long run equilibrium of a firm under monopolistic competition is achieved when the demand curve (LAR_{MC}) becomes tangential to the LAC curve at point F so that it earns only normal profits. Under such circumstances, a firm can reduce AC (and hence price) by expanding output to the minimum level of LAC, but it will not because its profits are maximised (equality of MR with rising MC is attained) at the level of output smaller than that at which its LAC is minimum.

Society's productive resources are fully utilised when they are used to produce the level of output which renders LAC minimum. Thus a monopolistically competitive firm produces less (OQ_{MC}) than the socially optimum or ideal output i.e. the output corresponding to the lowest point of the AC curve. This is in sharp contrast to the position of the firms in long-run equilibrium under perfect competition which operates at the minimum point of the LAC curve. The output produced under perfect competition is OQ_{PC}. The amount by which the actual long run output of the firm under monopolistic competition falls short of the socially ideal output is a measure of excess capacity which lies unutilised (distance between Q_{MC} and Q_{PC}).

It can be observed from the diagram (Fig. 3.17) that a firm under perfect competition produces socially ideal output whereas a monopolistic competitive firm can expand its production and reduce its LAC to its minimum.

This excess capacity is the peculiarity of monopolistic competition. The surplus capacity is never cast off, and the result is high prices and wastes. According to Chamberlin, the theory of monopolistic competition "affords an explanation of such wastes in an economic system - wastes which are normally referred to as 'wastes of competition'. In fact they could never occur under perfect competition. They are wastes of monopoly: of the monopoly elements in monopolistic competition."

3.4 OLIGOPOLY

Oligopoly is an important form of imperfect competition. Oligopoly prevails when there are **few firms** or sellers in the market producing or selling a product. In this case we find a **small number of big firms, whose products may or may not be differentiated.**

Oligopoly is defined as the market structure in which there are a few sellers of the homogeneous or differentiated products, who intensely compete against each other and recognise interdependence in their decision making. Oligopoly is often referred to as **'Competition among the few'.** The oligopoly model fits well into such industries as auto-mobile, manufacturing of electrical appliances, tyres, computers air conditioners, aluminium etc.

When the products of few sellers are homogeneous, it is called 'pure oligopoly' and when the products of the few sellers or firms are differentiated and are close substitutes of each other, 'differentiated oligopoly' is said to prevail.

Characteristics

1. **Few sellers:** There are a few sellers in the market selling either homogeneous or differentiated products. Each seller has sizeable influence on the market. Every firm possesses a large degree of monopoly power (when products are differentiated) and accounts for a large part of market's total demand. It uses all resources at its disposal to counter the actions of rival firms to ensure survival and growth in the market. Thus each firm acts as a strategic competitor.
2. **Interdependence:** The most important feature of oligopoly is the **interdependence in decision-making** of the few firms

which comprise the industry. This is because when the number of competitors is few, any change in price, output, product etc. by a firm will have a direct effect on the fortune of its rival, which will then retaliate in changing their own prices, output or products as the case may be. It is therefore clear that the oligopolistic firm must consider not only the market demand for the industry's product but also the reaction of the other firms in the industry to any action or decision it may take. Since more than one reaction pattern is possible from the other firms, it is necessary that some assumptions about the reactions of the others is made before a definite and determinate solution of price output fixation is provided under oligopoly.

Suppose, a firm starts a massive advertising campaign or designs a new model of his product, which captures the market. This policy change on the part of the firm will have obvious and immediate effects on its competitors. The competitors are likely to react with counter policies to avoid drifting off of its customers to other firms. Now, the former firm may have to react. This process of action-reaction of the firms may continue in an unending phase of uncertainty.

3. **Importance of advertising and selling costs:** With high cross elasticity of demand for the product under oligopoly, the oligopolist can raise his sales through non-price competition either by advertising his product or by improving its quality. Both these tools shift the demand in favour of the product and increase the market share of an oligopolistic firm. A direct effect of interdependence of oligopolists is that the various firms have to employ various aggressive and defensive marketing weapons to gain a greater share in the market or to prevent a fall in share. For this, various firms have to incur a good deal of costs on advertising and on other measures of sales promotion. Therefore there is a great importance of advertising and selling costs under conditions of market situation characterised by oligopoly. According to W. J. Baumol "it is only under oligopoly that advertising comes fully into its own. Under oligopoly, advertising can become a life and death matter, where a firm which fails to keep up with the advertising budget of its competitors may find its customers drifting off to rival products." In view of the fact that a firm in an oligopolistic industry competes by changing the

advertisement costs, quality of the product, prices, output etc., the presence of competitive conditions in it can hardly be derived.

4. **Group behaviour:** Another important feature of oligopoly is that for its proper solution, analysis of group behaviour is important i.e. whether the firms will co-operate to promote common objectives or compete against each other. There is no generally accepted theory of group behaviour.

   Unlike other market forms, the behaviour of a firm is unpredictable under oligopoly due to various reasons. *First,* the firms constituting the group may not have a common objective *Secondly,* the firms may enter into formal or informal collusion to achieve the profit maximization goal by avoiding uncertainty and ruinous rivalry. *Finally,* the group may be dominated by a leader.

5. **Indeterminateness of the demand curve facing an oligopolistic:** No firm under oligopoly faces a determinate demand curve on account of *interdependence* and *uncertainty.*

   The element of *interdependence* of firms has made the systematic analysis of oligopoly very difficult. The mutual interdependence also makes predictions and hence an optimal decision is very difficult due to the atmosphere of uncertainty. No firm under oligopoly is in a position to visualise the consequences of its price-output policy with any degree of accuracy.

   There is a high degree of *uncertainty* regarding which variable or combination of variables, the rival firm will use in its reaction pattern, in response to change in price, product variation and selling activities by the first firm. A wide variety of behaviour pattern becomes possible. Two conflicting attitudes on the part of the firms operate in the market. Sometimes, the firms realise the disadvantages of mutual competition and tend to collude to maximize their joint profits. At other times, the desire of each firm to earn maximum profits may reflect conflicts among firms.

   Indeterminateness of the demand curve facing an oligopolist is an important feature of oligopoly. The demand curve shows what amounts of its product a firm will be able to sell at various prices. Under oligopoly, a firm cannot assume that its rivals will keep their prices unchanged when it makes changes in its own price. As a result of this, the demand curve facing an oligopolistic firm loses its definiteness and determinateness, since it goes on constantly shifting as the rivals change their prices in reaction to price change by a firm.

6. **Price rigidity:** In an oligopolistic market, each firm sticks to its own price. This is because it is in constant fear of retaliation from rivals if it reduces the price. Therefore it resorts to advertisement competition than price cut. Hence there is price rigidity in an oligopolistic market.
7. **Kinked Demand Curve:** According to Paul Sweezy, firms in an oligopolistic market face a *kinked demand curve (or a kinked average revenue curve).* In a sense, there is no revenue function for an oligopolist at all. The amount he sells depends on the prices charged by other producers, and unless these can be specified in advance he cannot know what demand for his product will be. The *kinked* demand curve provides a simple way of conceiving an average revenue curve for an oligopolist which in turn helps us to understand oligopoly pricing problems.

A kinked demand curve is illustrated in Fig. 3.18

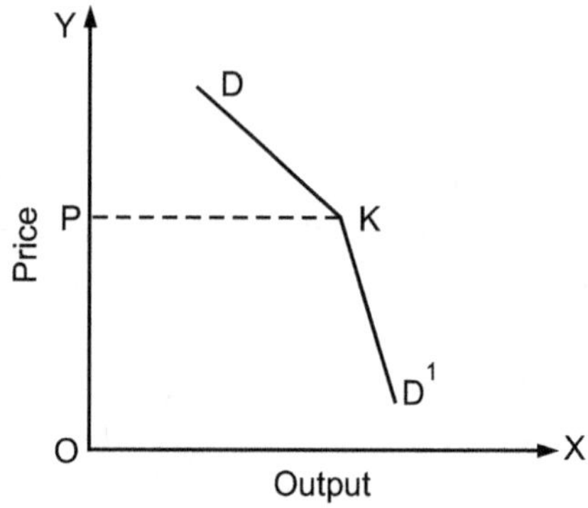

Fig. 3.18: Kinked Demand Curve

In Fig 3.18, the kinked demand curve or the average revenue curve is made of two segments:

(i) The relatively elastic demand curve: DK , where the demand curve is flatter and

(ii) The relatively inelastic demand curve: KD', where the demand curve is steep.

Corresponding to the given price OP, there is a kink at point K on the demand curve DD'. The kink implies an abrupt change in the slope of the demand curve.

The kink leads to indeterminateness of the course of demand for the product of the seller concerned. He thus, thinks it worthwhile to follow the prevailing price and not to make any change in it.

This is because, if he ***raises the price,*** **none of his competitors** follow (because they feel that a higher price would give too low a level of sales). Since the firms are producing very similar products, a small increase in the price of our seller's product will therefore lead to a very ***large fall in its sales***. Demand is *very elastic above the kink*, if one firm alone increases its price. Moreover, there is the fear of losing buyers to the rivals who do not raise their prices.

On the other hand, if he ***lowers the price,*** **it would lead to an immediate retaliation from the rivals** who will also cut their prices to the same extent. The rivals feel that while it may be unprofitable to cut prices, the danger that they will lose market share if they do not do so is too great for them to be able to allow our seller's price cuts to go unmatched. The result is that our seller will not expect much rise in his sales with price reduction. The demand curve below the kink is ***less elastic*** **if one firm reduces its price**.

Patterns of behaviour in an Oligopolistic Market

1. **Price leadership**: A traditional leader in the oligopoly market announces price changes from time to time which other competitors follow. The dominant firm may assume the price leadership. There is **barometric price leadership** when a smaller firm tries out a new price, which may or may not be recognised by the larger firms. The price leadership of a firm depends on a number of factors such as dominance in the market, initiative, aggressive pricing and reputation.
2. **Price wars:** Under cut-throat competition among the rivals, price wars may emerge in an oligopolistic market. Under price wars, firms tend to charge prices even below their variable cost. Price wars are never planned. They occur as a consequence when one firm cuts the prices and others following suit.
3. **Price cuts to weed out competition:** A financially strong firm may deliberately resort to price cuts to eliminate competitors from the market and secure its position.
4. **Collusion**: Business syndicates or trusts may be formed by the competing firms and they may agree to charge a uniform price, thereby to eliminate price retaliation or price cut competition.

Such business collusion implies conversion of an oligopoly into a monopoly. Business collusion is considered illegal under anti-trust laws.

5. **Secret Price Concessions:** Sometimes, oligopolists may offer secret price concessions for selected buyers instead of having an open price cut, which is likely to be retaliated by their rivals.
6. **Non-price competition:** Owing to the danger of retaliation in price cut competition, the oligopolists may also resort to non-price competition by competing in sales promotion efforts, advertising, product improvement etc. Here, too, the rivals retaliate.

3.5 DUOPOLY

So far, we have discussed market structures in which there were very large number of sellers as in perfect competition, a single seller or a single group of individuals who dominate the entire market as in monopoly and many sellers (but not as many as in perfect competition) competing with each other as in monopolistic competition , few sellers competing with each other as in oligopoly.

The simplest analytical form of oligopoly is duopoly. When there are two monopolists instead of one who share the monopoly power, it is called Duopoly. This is also a special form of oligopoly because from the point of view of the price theory the nature of the problem is the same whether there are two or few sellers.

There are three classical duopoly models given by Cournot (A.A. Cournot, French economist, 1838), Edgeworth (F.Y. Edgeworth) and Chamberlin (E.H. Chamberlin). These models employ simplified assumptions about interdependence of decision-making between the two firms. The first two models are drastically simplified by assuming that in deciding his price-output policy, one duopolist does not take into consideration the possible reactions which his rival may have to his actions. This assumption of ignoring completely the mutual interdependence of two rivals has been called Zero Conjectural Variation (Fritz Machlup). Chamberlin however has not ignored this problem.

Duopoly are of two types:

(a) Duopoly without Product Differentiation and

(b) Duopoly with Product Differentiation.

(a) Duopoly without product differentiation: Under duopoly the simplest cases will be those where the two monopolists are supposed to be selling an identical commodity and there is no product differentiation.

It is very likely that there will be collusion between the two. They may agree on a price or assign quotas or divide the territory in which each is to market his goods. This is possible if their respective cost curves are at least nearly identical, and if the demand is stable and less elastic. This collusion creates conditions almost similar to a monopoly and the price determination will be similar to that under monopoly.

However, in case there is no agreement between the two, a constant price war will occur. In this case the important factors to be considered are the costs and gains in driving out the rival, the relative sizes of the two firms, the demand elasticity and mobility of the purchasers, the promptness with which the rival reacts to changes in the other's policy and the extent to which price concession can be kept secret and so on.

When there is no product differentiation and goods are identical, the consumers are indifferent between the two producers and the same price must be charged by both in the long run, otherwise the one charging more will be wiped out of the market. They must fix a price as if they were a single monopolist rolled in one. Only then they will be able to maximise profits.

In case there is a price war between them, they will be able to earn only normal profits as under perfect competition. If their costs are different, the one with lower cost will wipe out the other and a single monopoly would be established. The best course for the duopolists will be to fix the monopoly price and share the market and profits.

It is possible that in the short run, duopoly price may be lower than the competitive price, none of the producers earning normal profits. In the long run this price may be somewhere between the monopoly price and the competitive price.

(b) Duopoly with product differentiation: When there is product differentiation, each producer has his own clientele and goodwill. There is no fear of immediate retaliatory measures by the rivals, if one producer changes his price output policy. There is less danger of price war. There will be no agreement between them. Since products are not similar, the firm with better products can earn supernormal profits.

3.6 COMPARISON OF PERFECT AND IMPERFECT COMPETITION

We have already discussed earlier how a monopoly firm generates excess capacity and have seen that perfect competition ensures the most efficient allocation of resources. Let us extend that discussion to monopolistic competition, by making a comparative evaluation of allocation of resources by monopolistic competition, perfect competition and monopoly.

Fig. 3.19 compares long run equilibrium of three firms, the first under perfect competition, the second under monopolistic competition, and the third under monopoly. All the firms are in a state of equilibrium and are earning normal profits. The firm under perfect competition faces a horizontal demand curve (D_C) and produces an output Q_C at price P_C. The monopolistically competitive firm faces a downward sloping demand curve (D_{MC}); it produces an output Q_{MC} (less than Q_C), at price P_{MC} (more than P_C). The monopolist firm also faces a downward sloping curve D_M, which is less elastic than D_{MC} and produces an output Q_M (less than Q_C and Q_{MC}), at price P_M (more than P_C and P_{MC}). We can thus infer that a monopolistically competitive firm produces (or sells) lesser at higher price as compared to a firm operating under perfect competition, and a monopoly firm produces and sells less than both firms under monopolistic and perfect competition. The difference in output, shown as $Q_C - Q_M$ and also $Q_C - Q_{MC}$ is known as excess capacity. A firm under monopoly or monopolistic competition would produce at a level of output where AC and its demand curve are still declining (i.e. to the left of point E_M and E_{MC}). Thus, it produces with excess capacity. In fact, no firm, either in monopolistic competition or in monopoly, would operate at the minimum point on its AC curve. Now each firm's demand curve is downward sloping. As such, it is tangent to the AC curve at some point above the minimum point of AC curve. In other words, a monopolist as well as a monopolistically competitive firm operate at less than optimum output and charge a higher price. It is for this reason that many economists consider a monopolistically competitive firm to be inefficient and exclude monopoly practices from good economics.

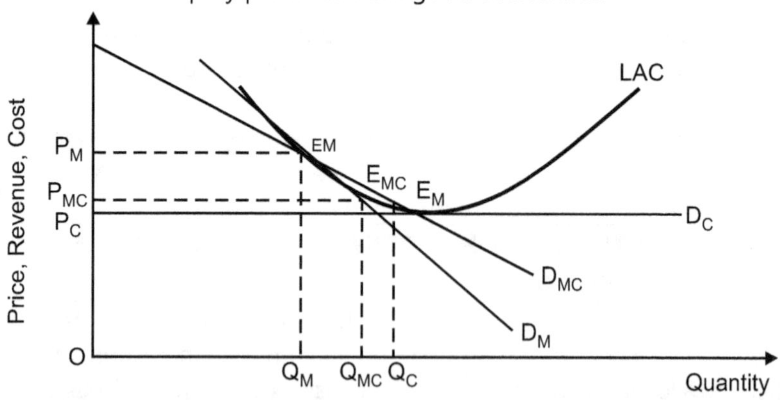

Fig. 3.19: Excess Capacity under Monopolistic Competition and Monopoly

However, we should also remember that due to the presence of a large number of substitutes, the demand curve of a monopolistically competitive firm is highly elastic. As such, the price difference between monopolistic competition and perfect competition may not be appreciable. Moreover, consumers get a wide variety of competing brands to choose from, unlike prefect competition, in which the product is homogeneous. Thus, the loss is welfare due to higher price and lower output is counter balanced by a gain in satisfaction due to wider choices. However, none of these arguments are valid in the case of monopoly, hence all regulatory authorities make regulations to check and prevent monopoly practices.

POINTS TO REMEMBER

1. **Imperfect competition:**
   The real life situation is of imperfect competition where there is neither perfect competition nor absolute monopoly. This market situation is also known as **Monopolistic Competition.**
2. **Monopoly: Meaning and Types** - The term monopoly is derived from 'mono' (single) and 'poly' (selling). Thus 'monopoly' means a single control over the supply of output. Monopoly is that market form in which a single producer controls the entire supply of a commodity which has very few substitutes or no substitutes at all.
3. **Types of Monopoly:**
   (a) Pure Monopoly and Imperfect Monopoly: Pure Monopoly means a single firm which controls the supply of a commodity which has no substitutes. It possesses absolute monopoly power. Such a monopoly is rare.
   Imperfect Monopoly means a limited degree of monopoly. It refers to a single firm which produces a commodity having no close substitutes.
   (b) Legal, Natural, Technological and Joint Monopolies:
      (i) Legal monopolies emerge on account of legal provisions like patents, trademarks, copyrights etc.
      (ii) Natural advantages like good location, old-age establishment, involvement of huge investment, business reputation etc confer natural monopolies on many firms.
      (iii) Technological expertise, economies of large scale and efficiency of superior capital use and the process of mechanization etc., confer technological monopolies to big firms.
      (iv) Through business combinations like trusts, cartels, syndicates etc., some firms may unite in a group and acquire joint monopolies in the market.

(c) **Simple Monopoly and Discriminating Monopoly:** A simple monopoly firm charges a uniform price for its product to all the buyers. It operates in a single market.
A discriminating monopoly firm charges different prices for the same product to different buyers. It operates in more than one market.

(d) **Private Monopoly and Public or Social Monopoly:** Considering the nature of ownership, monopolies may be grouped into:
Private monopolies: when an individual or a private body controls a monopoly firm, it is regarded as a private monopoly.
Public or Social Monopoly: when production is solely owned, controlled and operated by the state, it is regarded as a social or public monopoly.

4. **Monopoly equilibrium in the short-run:**
(a) SNP (AR > AC), (b) NP (AR = AC), (c) Loss (AR < AC)

5. **Monopoly equilibrium in the long-run:**
(a) Case of SNP (LAR > LAC), (b) Case of NP (LAR = LAC)

6. Price discrimination is profitable only if elasticity of demand in one market is different from the elasticity of demand in the other.

7. **Features of monopolistic competition:**
(a) Large no of sellers
(b) Freedom of entry and exit of firm
(c) Product differentiation
(d) Selling costs/Sales promotion
(e) Concept of group
(f) Price competition on non-price competition

8. **Product Differentiation:** A general class of product is differentiated if a basis exists for preferring goods of one seller to those of another. Such a basis for preference may be real or fancied, but it will cause differentiation of the product.

9. **Oligopoly** is an important form of imperfect competition where we find a small number of big firms, whose products may or may not be differentiated.

10. **Characteristics of Oligopoly:**
(a) Few sellers, (b) Interdependence, (c) Importance of advertising and selling costs, (d) Group behaviour, (e) Indeterminate of the demand curve, (f) Price rigidity, (g) Kinked Demand Curve.

11. **Duopoly:**
    When there are two monopolists instead of one who share the monopoly power, it is called Duopoly.
12. **Characteristics of Duopoly:**
    (a) Duopoly without product differentiation
    (b) Duopoly with product differentiation.

QUESTIONS FOR DISCUSSION

1. What is Imperfect Competition?
2. Define Monopoly. Explain the features of monopoly.
3. Elaborate on the causes of monopoly.
4. How is output determined under monopoly?
5. Describe monopoly equilibrium in the short run.
6. Describe monopoly equilibrium in the long run.
7. Point out the similarities and differences between perfect competition and monopoly.
8. What is Price Discrimination or who is a Discriminating monopoly?
9. Describe the various forms of price discrimination?
10. When is price discrimination possible?
11. What are the degrees of price discrimination?
12. When is price discrimination profitable?
13. Describe the equilibrium of a discriminating monopolist.
14. What is monopolistic Competition? Explain its features.
15. Describe the short run equilibrium of a firm under monopolistic competition.
16. Describe the long run equilibrium of a firm under monopolistic competition.
17. What is product differentiation?
18. Describe the two bases of product differentiation.
19. Write a note on selling costs.
20. Distinguish between selling cost and production cost.
21. Describe the equilibrium of a firm under monopolistic competition which incurs advertising expenses.
22. Explain excess capacity as a waste of monopolistic competition.
23. What is Oligopoly? What are the features of Oligopoly?
24. What is Duopoly? What are the features of Duopoly?

QUESTIONS FROM PAST EXAMINATIONS

1. What is Monopoly? **[April 2009]**
2. Define Price Discrimination. **[April 2009, Oct. 2010]**
   OR
   What is Price Discrimination? **[Oct. 2009]**

3. Define Oligopoly. **[Oct. 2009, April 2010]**
4. What is Monopolistic Competition? **[April 2010]**
5. State features of Oligopoly. **[April 2009, 2012, Oct. 2010]**
6. Write Short Note: Price Discrimination. **[April 2011]**
7. Explain the Price Determination under Monopolistic Competition. **[April 2006]**
8. Explain the Price Determination under Monopolistic Competition in the short-run. **[Oct. 2006]**
9. What are the Features of Monopolistic Competition? Explain the Price Determination under Monopolistic Competition. **[April 2008]**
10. What is Monopoly? Explain Price Determination under Monopoly. **[Oct. 2010]**
11. State the features of oligopoly. **[April 2012]**
12. Features of monopolistic competition. **[April 2013]**
13. State the Types of Monopoly. **[April 2006]**
14. State the Characteristics of Oligopoly. **[Oct. 2006]**
15. Explain the Features of Monopoly. **[Oct. 2007]**
16. Explain the Price Determination under Monopolistic Competition. **[April 2006]**
17. What are the features of Monopolistic Competition? Explain the Equilibrium of the Firm under the Monopolistic Competition. **[April 2014, 2016; Oct. 2015]**
18. State the Features of Oligopoly. **[April 2009, 2012, 2014, 2018; Oct. 2010, 2016, 2017]**
19. What is Monopoly? Explain Price Determination under Monopoly. **[Oct. 2010]**
20. State the Features of Monopolistic Competition. **[Oct. 2016]**
21. State the Features of Monopoly. **[April 2017]**
22. Write Short Notes:
    - **(A)** Types of Price Discrimination. **[April 2014, Oct. 2015]**
    - **(B)** Features of Oligopoly. **[April 2015, 2016, 2017]**
    - **(C)** Features of Monopoly. **[Oct. 2015]**
    - **(D)** Features of Monopolistic Competition. **[April 2017]**
    - **(E)** Price Discrimination. **[April 2012, 2017, Oct. 2016]**

Unit **4**...

Factor Pricing

Contents ...

Learning Objectives ...

- To discuss Marginal Productivity theory of Distribution
- To know what is rent and understand the various theories of rent like Ricardian theory and Modern Theory of Rent and the Concept of Quasi Rent
- To understand wages, types of wages, the backward bending supply curve of labour and collective bargaining
- To learn about interest and theories of interest
- To elaborate on the concept of Profit and various theories of profit

4.1 MARGINAL PRODUCTIVITY THEORY

The preceding chapters were concerned with the pricing and output of goods and services under a variety of product market structures. In producing any commodity, a firm must hire productive resources which, directly or indirectly, are owned and supplied by households. It is appropriate that we now turn from the pricing and production of goods to the pricing and employment of resources needed in accomplishing production. In terms of our circular flow diagram of the economy (Ch 1: Sem. I), we now shift our attention from the bottom loop of the diagram, where firms supply and households demand products, to the top loop, where households supply and businesses demand resources. Hence, there is a need for a separate discussion on resource pricing or factor pricing.

The factors of production, namely land, labour, capital and enterprise provide their productive service or participate in production activity and create national wealth. This national wealth in turn is distributed among the factors of production in the form of rent, wages, interest and profit as remuneration for their contribution to production activity. Thus *distribution* means the sharing of the wealth that is produced among the different factors of production. There are two aspects of the distribution process.

- **(i) Functional Distribution:** This is the share of the factors of production in the form of rent, wages, and interest and profits in the aggregate production. It deals with the reward for unique functions rendered by the factors of production through their productive services.
- **(ii) Personal Distribution:** This refers to a given amount of wealth and income received by individuals in society through their economic efforts i.e. an individual's personal earnings through various sources.

The theory of distribution deals with **functional distribution** and not with **personal distribution.** It deals with the evaluation of the services of the factors of production: the principles governing the determination of factor rewards: rent, wages, interest and profits i.e. how the prices of the factors of production are set.

4.2 MARGINAL PRODUCTIVITY THEORY OF DISTRIBUTION

The **marginal productivity theory of distribution** also known as the **General Theory of Distribution** has been propounded by the neo-classical school. J. B. Clark, Jevons, Marshall and Hicks have made important contributions to the development of this theory. The theory was initially propounded as an explanation for determining wages but later generalised as a theory of factor pricing for all factors of production.

The theory states that the price of a factor of production is governed by its marginal productivity. The theory analyses the process of equilibrium in the factor market under perfect competitive conditions. When there is perfect competition in the factor market, the firm can employ any number of factor units at the prevailing market price. The firm will employ that many factor units (or it will maximise profits) or will be in equilibrium at that point where the marginal productivity of the factors is equal to its price. Hence, the price or return of the factor equals its marginal productivity.

Before we discuss the marginal productivity theory of distribution in detail let us understand some of the important **concepts** used in this theory:

(I) Productivity of a factor can be expressed in two ways:

(i) Physical productivity.

(ii) Revenue productivity.

(i) Physical productivity: In this case productivity is expressed in physical terms - in terms of physical units of a commodity. Further physical productivity has two parts:

(a) Average physical product (APP): also known as Average product: This is the ratio of total product to the number of units of factor. I.e. APP = TP/n

Where TP = Total product

n = number of units of factor.

(b) Marginal physical product (MPP): also known as Marginal Product: This measures the increase in total product as a result of employment of an additional unit of factor. i.e.

$$MPP_n = TP_n: TP_{n-1}$$

The concepts of APP and MPP can be clarified with the help of the following table:

Table 4.1

No of units of labour Employed	**Total Physical Product TPP (in units, kg)**	**Average Physical Product- APP (in units, kg)**	**Marginal Physical Product MPP (in units, kg)**
1	8	8	8
2	17	8.5	9
3	27	9	10
4	38	9.5	11
5	35	9	7
6	51	8.5	6
7	56	8	5

It has been assumed in the above table that all units of labour from 1 to 7 are homogeneous. It can be observed that APP as well as MPP both increase till 4 units of labour is employed. This is because of the law of increasing returns. After the 5th unit of labour, both APP and MPP begin to decline. This is because of the law of diminishing returns.

(ii) Revenue productivity: When physical productivity is expressed in monetary terms it is known as revenue productivity. Further revenue productivity can be divided into

(a) Average Revenue Productivity (ARP): also known as **average productivity** of a factor: This is the ratio of total revenue to the number of factor units employed

i.e. $$ARP = \frac{TR}{n}$$

OR

$$ARP = APP \times Price\ (AR)$$

(b) Marginal Revenue Product (MRP): This measures the increase in total revenue as a result of employment of an additional unit of factor.

i.e. $$MRP = TR_n : TR_{n-1}$$

OR

$$MRP = MPP \times MR$$

Under perfect competition MR = AR

Hence $$MRP = MPP_x\ Price\ (AR)$$

This can be explained with the help of Table 4.2.

Table 4.2

No of units of labour employed	Price (AR=MR)	Marginal Physical Product (MPP × Price)	Marginal Revenue Product (MRP) (MPP × Price)	Average Physical Product (APP)	Average Revenue Product (ARP) (APP × Price)
1	2	8	16	8	16
2	2	9	18	8.5	17
3	2	10	20	9	18
4	2	11	22	9.5	19
5	2	7	14	9	18
6	2	6	12	8.5	17
7	2	5	10	8	16

The above Table 4.2 can be translated into the following Fig. 4.1.

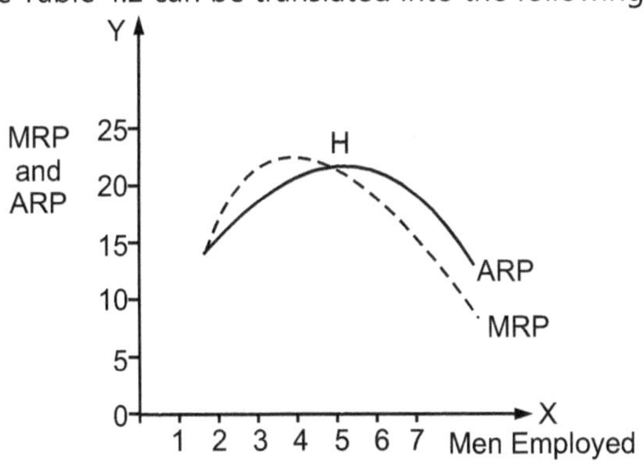

Fig. 4.1

In Fig. 4.1, it can be seen that the curves ARP and MRP have an inverted U shape. The relation between ARP and MRP is the same as between average and marginal cost, namely

(i) When ARP rises, MRP lies above it;

(ii) When ARP reaches its maximum, MRP = ARP.

(iii) When ARP declines, MRP lies below it.

The MRP is the producer's demand curve for the factor (say labour).

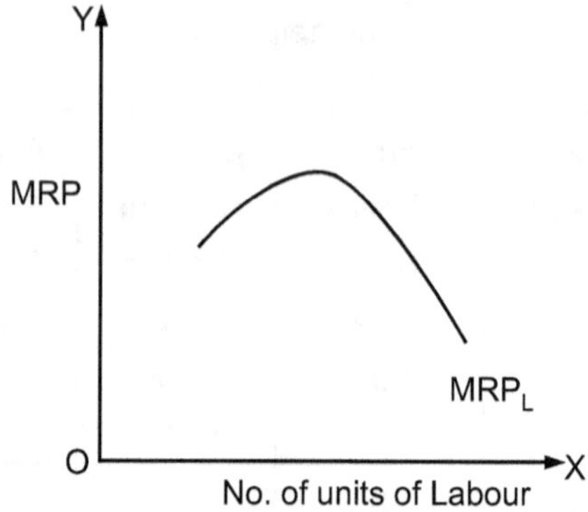

Fig. 4.2

In Fig. 4.2 it can be seen that as the number of units of labour increases, MRP declines. Therefore an employer will be willing to pay lower wages for increasing levels of employment.

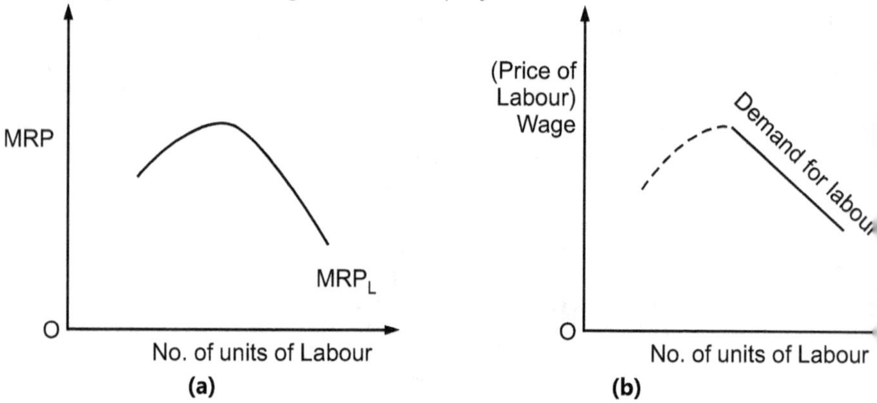

Fig. 4.3

Fig. 4.3 (a) represents MRP of labour which has an inverted U shape. In Fig. 4.3 (b) we have the demand curve for labour which is derived from MRP_L in Fig. 4.3 (a). The demand for labour is downward sloping indicating that the producer will employ more units of labour only at lower wages.

Concepts of Factor Cost

Average Factor Cost and Marginal Factor Cost (AFC and MFC)

The price paid by the firm to a factor of production, say labour is the cost of production to the firm. When there is perfect competition in the factor market, the price of the factor is determined by the forces of demand and supply of that factor. Hence at the prevailing price, any amount of the factor can be employed. Thus from the firm's point of view, the **supply of a factor is perfectly elastic** at the given factor price. As a result the average factor cost (AFC) and the marginal factor cost (MFC) of the factor to the firm are equal to the price of that factor i.e. AFC = MFC = price of the factor. This can be understood with the help of the following table and diagram.

Table 4.3

Labour (L)	Wages (W)	Total Wages (= W × L)	Average Wages $\frac{TW}{L}$	Marginal Wages $\left(\frac{\Delta TW}{\Delta L}\right)$
1	10	10	10	–
2	10	20	10	10
3	10	30	10	10
4	10	40	10	10
5	10	50	10	10

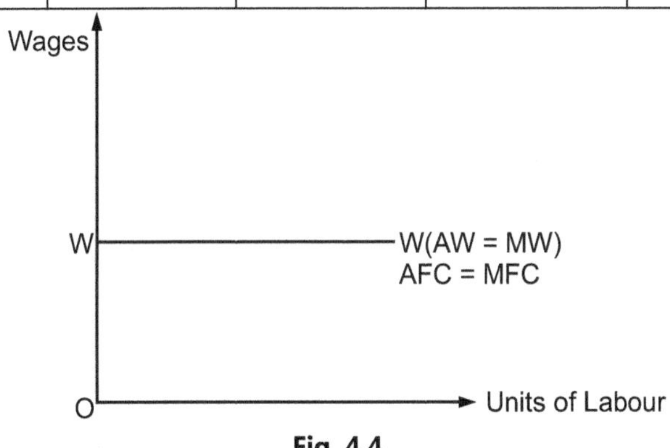

Fig. 4.4

At the prevailing factor price, the individual firm can employ any amount of factor it desires. Since the factor price is assumed as given and constant, AFC = MFC and is represented by a horizontal line parallel to the X-axis. WW is the supply curve of labour which is perfectly elastic.

Assumptions of the Marginal Productivity Theory

1. It is assumed that there is perfect competition in the factor and product market.
2. It is assumed that technology remains constant.
3. It is assumed that all units of factor are perfectly homogeneous i.e. they are of equal efficiency.
4. It is assumed that the objective of the firm is profit maximisation.
5. It is assumed that there is full employment of resources.

6. It is assumed that factors of production are perfectly mobile.
7. It is assumed that the buyers and sellers of factors of production have equal bargaining power.
8. There is no government intervention in the form of minimum wages legislation etc.
9. It is assumed that the marginal productivity of a factor is measurable.

Equilibrium in the Factor Market:

Given the demand and supply conditions of the factor, the firm will continue to employ more and more units of a particular factor so long as additional revenue obtained from an additional unit of the factor (MRP) exceeds the additional cost of employing it (MFC). It will be earning maximum profits at the point at which MRP = MFC. If the firm employs less than this, MRP would be higher than MFC and it would be to its advantage to hire more units of the factor because they would add to revenue than to costs. In case the firm decides to hire beyond the point of equality of MRP and MFC, it would be a loser because costs would rise more than revenue. Thus in a **perfectly competitive factor market, a firm will be in equilibrium** when the following **two conditions** are satisfied -

(i) MRP = MFC
(ii) MRP curve must cut the MFC curve from above at the equilibrium point.

This can be illustrated as follows:

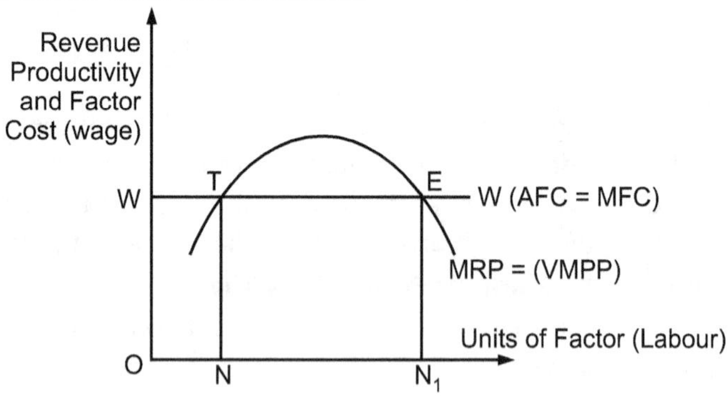

Fig. 4.5

In the above Fig. 4.5, it can be seen that given wage rate OW, the firm will employ labour units till wages (OW) = MRP (at point E) i.e. it will employ ON_1 units of labour where its profits will be maximised. If it employs labour less than ON_1 units (e.g. ON units) it is possible for the firm to increase profits by increasing labour employment upto ON_1 [because MRP > Wage rate (MFC)]. If the firm employs labour greater than ON_1 units of labour, its profits are less than maximum [because MRP < Wage rate (MFC)]. Therefore under perfectly competitive market conditions in the factor market, a firm will be in equilibrium with regard to employment of labour (factor) when marginal productivity or MRP of labour (factor) = MFC or wage rate. Further equilibrium is possible if MRP curve cuts MFC curve from above (point E and not point T). Hence in the **short run the price of the factor equals marginal productivity.**

From the above diagram it is not clear as to whether a firm makes a profit or incurs a loss and how much profit or loss it incurs. Hence we have to consider the long run equilibrium.

Long run Equilibrium in the Factor Market

Though a firm may be in equilibrium when MRP = MFC and MRP cuts MFC from above it does not imply that the industry is in equilibrium. This is because if the firms are earning super normal profits (SNPs), new firms will enter the industry and hence the demand for labour (factor) will increase. Wage rate will thus rise and the AFC = MFC curve shifts upward. If some firms are incurring losses, they quit the industry and therefore demand for labour (factor) will fall. Wage rate will thus fall and the AFC = MFC curve will shift downwards. This increase or decrease in wage rate will cease when all the firms are earning only normal profits where ARP = AFC = MRP = MFC. This can be illustrated as follows:

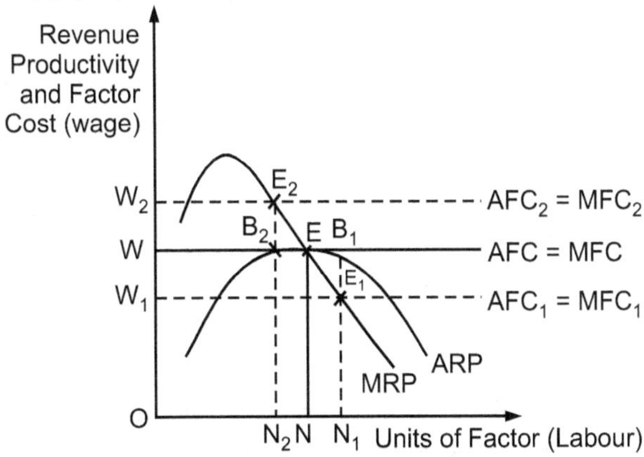

Fig. 4.6

In the above Fig. 4.6, let OW_1 be the wage rate determined by the market forces of demand and supply of labour. The firm is in equilibrium at E_1 and it employs ON_1 units of labour. In this situation ARP > AFC (i.e. B_1N_1 > E_1N_1) and supernormal profits (B_1E_1 per unit) prevail. Therefore new firms enter. The demand for labour rises and the wage rate rises to say OW_2. When the wage rate is OW_2 the firm is in equilibrium at E_2 and it employs ON_2 units of labour. In this situation ARP < AFC (i.e. B_2N_2 < E_2N_2) and the firm incurs loss (E_2B_2 per unit). Therefore some firms quit. The demand for labour falls and the wage rate falls.

Finally the industry will be in equilibrium in the long run when all the firms earn only normal profits. I.e. when wage rate = OW and ARP is tangential to AFC = MFC curve. The firm is at equilibrium at point E and employs ON units of labour.

Here Wage = AFC = MFC = MRP = ARP.

Therefore in the long run, wage rate = MRP = ARP.

Hence in the **long run,** the **price of a factor equals marginal productivity which equals average productivity.**

Criticism of the Marginal Productivity Theory of Distribution

1. The assumptions underlying the theory are unrealistic-
   (a) Perfect competition is not a very realistic phenomenon.
   (b) Since it assumes technology to be constant, it can be applicable only to a static economy. In a dynamic economy, technology advances from time to time. Therefore this theory is highly inapplicable to modern conditions.
   (c) Factor units are never alike: labour units differ in efficiency and skill: so does land in fertility.
   (d) It is found that profit maximisation is not the sole objective of a firm: the firm's objective can also be sales maximisation, enhancing social welfare etc.
   (e) As Keynes pointed out underemployment situation is more likely than full employment of factors.
   (f) Factors are quite immobile between regions and occupations.
   (g) Critics point out that one cannot measure the marginal productivity of each factor separately because variation in output cannot be attributed to a single factor alone.
2. The theory basically explains wage determination and it has been extended to determine the prices of other factors of production. But it has to be noted that every factor has its own distinctive

characteristics and their rewards are also fixed distinctly. For example an entrepreneur's profit is considered to be a residual income and therefore it cannot be negative (loss). That this loss is because his marginal productivity was negative cannot be accepted.

3. The theory is one-sided. It explains how a factor reward is determined by its marginal productivity. However, it assumes a given factors price. Hence, it only analyses the demand side of the factor pricing and does not provide adequate explanation on the supply side.

4.3 RENT

Meaning of Rent

Economists use the term 'rent' in a narrow sense. They use the term **'economic rent':** that part of the payment which is made for the use of land only. It is defined as the price paid for the use of land and other natural resources which are completely fixed in total supply. It is the unique supply conditions of land and other natural resources: their fixed supply: which makes rental payments distinguishable from wages, interest and profit payments.

There are three theories of Rent:

1. **Ricardian Theory of Rent (also known as the Classical Theory of Rent):** In this theory rent is treated as a differential surplus accruing to land alone.
2. **Modern Theory of Rent (attributed mainly to Joan Robinson):** In this theory rent is earned by all factors of production. Here the concepts discussed are:
   (a) Scarcity rent
   (b) Rent as a generalised surplus
   (c) Difference between factors' actual earnings and its transfer earnings.
3. **Quasi Rent (attributed to Marshall):** In this, rent refers to short run earnings of some factors of production because they are fixed in supply during the short-run.

1. Ricardian Theory of Rent

According to Ricardo, rent is "that portion of the produce of the earth which is paid to the landlord for the use of the original and indestructible powers of the soil."

For greater understanding of the Ricardian model of rent formation, we first understand the various assumptions made by him:

(a) Ricardo considers the supply of land as completely fixed i.e. perfectly inelastic in supply.

(b) He does not take into account the various alternative uses to which land can put. He assumes the land to be used for growing a single composite crop, 'corn'

(c) He assumes that there is perfect competition in the market for land.

(d) He assumes that land differs in quality. There are various grades of land, differing from each other in respect of fertility and location. These differences in fertility lead to the factor yielding rent, i.e. Superior and more fertile lands yield a surplus due to their differential advantages in production over inferior or less fertile ones. Ricardo viewed rent as a 'differential surplus earned by more fertile plots of land in comparison with the less fertile plots of land. Therefore, Ricardian theory of rent is also called the differential theory of rent.

The emergence of differential rent in the Ricardian theory can be easily explained by imagining that a new island is discovered and some people come to settle there. There are only 4 plots of land A, B, C, D labelled in order of their fertility i.e. A is the most fertile plot, B is inferior to A, C is inferior to B and D is the least fertile land. It is assumed that corn is being cultivated and that the same doses of labour (L) and capital (K) are being used on these plots.

When people first come to this island, they will take up the best grade land A, for production of corn. So long as some of grade A land is yet lying idle, there will be no rent.

Let the initial demand for corn be 100 quintals, and let us suppose cultivation of Land A is sufficient to meet demand. But with the growth of population, as demand for food increases, say upto 170 quintals, the scarcity of land A is felt and inferior land B will be brought under cultivation. Now, the cost of cultivation of land A and B is same, yet land A yields 100 quintals of corn while land B yields only 70 quintals.

Therefore, land A releases a surplus of 30 quintals, over the yield of land B. It is a producer's surplus or it is a rent claimed by the owner of the land i.e. it is surplus of the superior land over inferior land.

If however, demand for food increases still further to say 220 quintals, land C will be brought under cultivation and with the same amount of labour and capital, land C yields 50 quintals of corn. Now, as compared to land C, land B yields a surplus of 20 quintals of corn (70 - 50) while land A yields a surplus of 50 quintals (100 - 50). As population continues to increase the demand for corn increases and land D will also be brought under cultivation. If land D yields 30 quintals of corn, then land A yields a surplus of 70 quintals, land B yields 40 quintals and land C also yields a surplus of 20 quintals. Thus land C which did not get any rent previously, also earns rent when an inferior quality of land is brought under cultivation. Expressing the analysis in money terms, we consider rent as the surplus over the cost of production. Let the cost of production (price of given amount of labour and capital) = ₹ 6000/-. Let corn cost ₹ 200/- per quintal. Rent yielded by different plots of land can be shown as follows:

Table 4.4

Land	**Price**	×	**Quantity**	=	**TR**	**TC**	**Surplus = TR – TC**
A	200	×	100	=	20,000	6000	14000
B	200	×	70	=	14000	6000	8000
C	200	×	50	=	10,000	6000	4000
D	200	×	30	=	6000	6000	-

Therefore according to Ricardo, the more fertile land yields more and more rent as more and more of less fertile land is brought under cultivation.

Ricardo describes the superior or more fertile land as intra-marginal land while less fertile land earning no rent is called the marginal land. The marginal land's revenue just covers its cost of cultivation and when still inferior land is brought under cultivation, the marginal land becomes intra-marginal land and starts earning rent. Thus

Differential rent or Surplus = Yields of Intra-Marginal land - Yield of Marginal land.

Differential rents can be diagrammatically represented as follows:

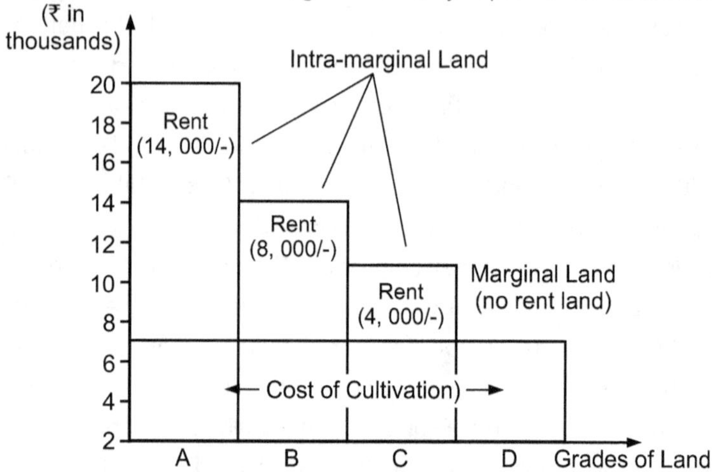

Fig. 4.7

The Ricardian theory of rent can also be explained with the help of a competitive market model of the equilibrium of the different forms, with different qualities of land. This is illustrated as follows:

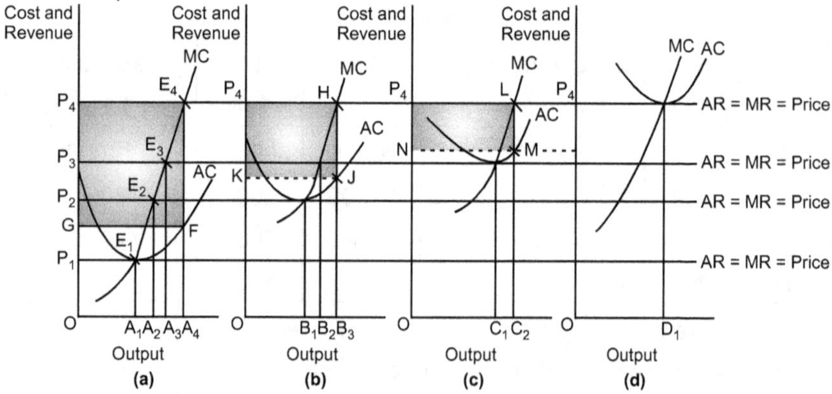

Fig. 4.8

In the Fig. 4.8, (a) represents the AC and MC curve of the most fertile land A, (b), (c), and (d) represents those of land B, C and D.

In the beginning, only land A is cultivated. OP_1 is the market price of corn and E_1 is the equilibrium point (MR= rising MC) and OA_1 of output is produced. Land A at this stage does not earn any rent as there is no surplus (Rent is the surplus revenue over cost).

When population increases and demand for corn rises, the price of corn increases to say OP_2. Now land B will also be cultivated and OB_1 will be cultivated in land B. In land A, equilibrium shifts to E_2 and OA_2 is cultivated. Since AR > AC, land A realises a surplus. This is the rent earned by the landlord of A.

Similarly, when population increases further and demand for corn rises, its price increases to OP_3. Land C is also brought under cultivation and now Land A earns greater surplus, therefore rent and land B also starts earning rent. And if price of corn rises to OP_4, (as a result of increase in demand due to rise in population) then land D is also cultivated - land A, B and C earn rent. A, B, and C are intra-marginal lands while D the no-rent land is the marginal land. (for D, AR = AC).

Rent for land A = P_4E_4FG

Rent for land B = P_4HJK

Rent for land C = P_4LMN

And land D earns no rent.

According to Ricardo, rent is **price-determined and not price-determining.** i.e. "corn is not high because a rent is paid, but a rent is paid because corn is high."

According to Ricardo, rent is a differential surplus of revenue over cost. This implies that rent is not treated as an element of cost. Now, price is based on AC and AC does not include rent. Therefore price does not depend on rent. Therefore **rent is not price-determining.** From the above analysis it is clear that as price of corn rises, rent also rises. Therefore rent depends on price.

Therefore **rent is price-determined.**

Criticism of the Ricardian Theory of Rent:

1. Ricardo's view of the concept of rent as a payment made for the use of original and indestructible powers of soil is incorrect. It is difficult to ascertain what these original powers are and what are not. Moreover, in the modern era, one cannot claim anything to be indestructible.
2. Ricardo assumed that land is cultivated in order of its fertility i.e. the most fertile land is cultivated first and then the less fertile land followed by the least fertile land. There is no empirical evidence in economic history to support this thesis. In fact it has been observed that location is more significant rather than fertility in its selection of cultivation.

3. The theory assumes perfect competition which is unrealistic.
4. In reality, if marginal land (no-rent land) does not exist, it is difficult to measure differential rent of intra-marginal land.
5. According to Ricardo, rent is a differential surplus accruing to land alone because of differences in fertility. But according to modern economists, rent would arise even if land was homogeneous. According to them, any factor (not just land) would earn rent if there exists an inelastic supply of that factor i.e. if the supply of a particular factor is less than perfectly elastic.

2. Modern Theory of Rent

The main propounder of the Modern Theory Of Rent is Mrs Joan Robinson. This theory is based on three important propositions:

(a) Rent arises due to scarcity of land.

(b) Rent is a generalised surplus earned by all factors.

(c) Rent, as a surplus, earned by a factor, is measured with reference to transfer earnings of the factor in its prevailing employment.

(a) Scarcity Rent

Here the determination of rent is explained in terms of the interaction of demand and supply forces. Rent is based on the scarcity of the availability of land: it is immaterial whether it is of superior or inferior or any other quality. Rent emerges even if all plots of land are homogeneous, if they are scarce in relation to demand.

According to the modern economists, in any period, whether long or short, the supply of land in existence is perfectly inelastic. Therefore a rise in demand for land, with the growth of population will intensify its relative scarcity, so the price of land i.e. rent, tends to rise further and further with the rise in demand. This is illustrated as follows:

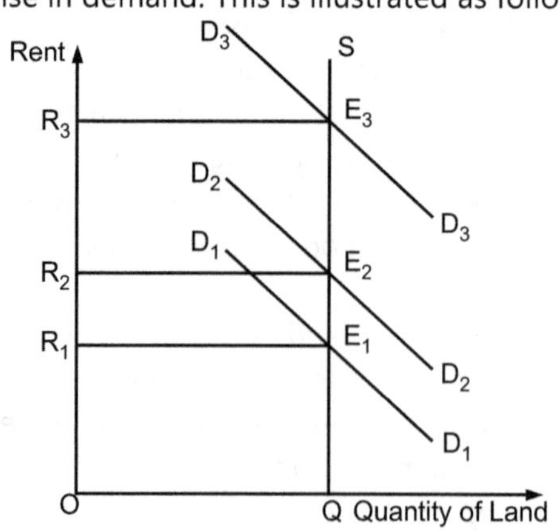

Fig. 4.9

In the above Fig. 4.9, SQ is the supply curve of land - perfectly inelastic. D_1D_1 is the initial demand curve for land and OR_1 is the equilibrium rent determined (where demand equals supply). If, however, demand increases, the new demand curve is D_2D_2 and rent increases to OR_2. Similarly a further shift in demand curve to D_3D_3 results in rent rising to OR_3.

Thus rent rises because of demand pressure and scarcity of land i.e. **scarcity rent is demand determined.**

(b) Rent as a Generalised Surplus

According to the modern economists, rent is a generalised surplus i.e. rent is not peculiar to land alone. It can be earned by any factor of production which is scarce in relation to its demand. Scarcity means inelasticity of supply and inelasticity of supply is not a peculiarity of land alone. Other factors of production like labour, capital and enterprise too are inelastic in supply at least in the short period. Therefore rent is a generalised surplus that can accrue to any factor of production.

(c) Measurement of Rent with reference to Transfer Earnings

According to Mrs Joan Robinson " the price which is necessary to retain a given unit of a factor in a certain industry may be called its **Transfer Earnings.**" (TEs)

TEs, in fact, are nothing but the opportunity cost of a factor i.e. what the factor could earn in its next best alternative use or employment is its TEs. In order to retain a factor in its particular use, it must be paid at least equal to its opportunity cost or TEs, i.e. what it could earn elsewhere. **The TEs are the minimum supply price of a factor unit in a particular industry.** The minimum supply price of a factor means the minimum payment which is necessary to induce him to continue to work in its present occupation.

Therefore

$$\text{Rent} = \begin{matrix}\text{Reward of a factor}\\ \text{in a particular industry}\end{matrix} - \begin{matrix}\text{The minimum supply price of that}\\ \text{factor in this industry}\end{matrix}$$

Further Minimum supply price of a factor unit in a particular industry = Transfer Earnings

Economic Rent = Current earning of a factor - its TE_S

According to the modern theory of rent, rent as a surplus over TEs depends on the elasticity of supply of the factor.

(i) Consider the case of a factor having perfectly inelastic supply. The TEs = 0 and the entire income is a surplus treated as rent. (In the case of land, it is a free gift of nature. Therefore its supply price = 0 or TE=0. Therefore the whole earnings are rent. Again, if land has only a specific use and cannot be used elsewhere, then also it's TE=0. Land moreover is perfectly inelastic in supply. Therefore when demand for land increases, rent increases proportionately. Therefore rent in the case of land remains completely a demand determined phenomenon).

This can be illustrated as follows:

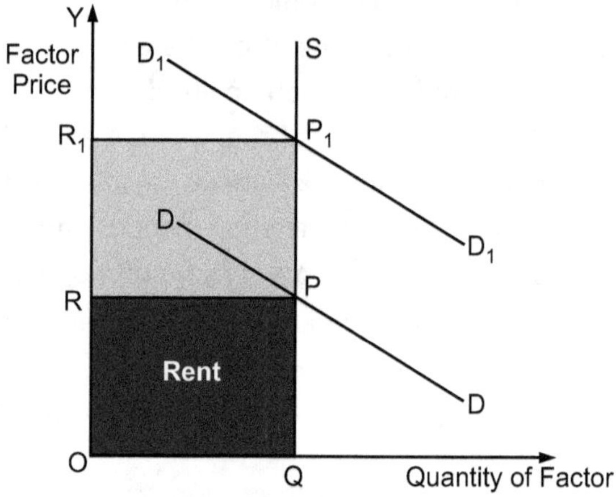

Fig. 4.10

In the above Fig. 4.10, given perfectly inelastic supply curve SQ and demand curve DD equilibrium factor price = OR and OQ is the number of factor units demanded and supplied. The total earnings of the factor = ORPQ. Since TEs = 0, the entire income is a differential surplus treated as rent When demand increases to D_1D_1, factor price equals OR_1 and total earnings also rises to OR_1P_1Q. Therefore rent increases when demand increases.

(ii) Consider the case of a factor with supply less than perfectly elastic

The supply curve in this case is upward sloping implying that additional units of the factor will be supplied only at higher prices. Hence, TEs (the minimum supply price) increases for each additional unit. This can be illustrated as follows:

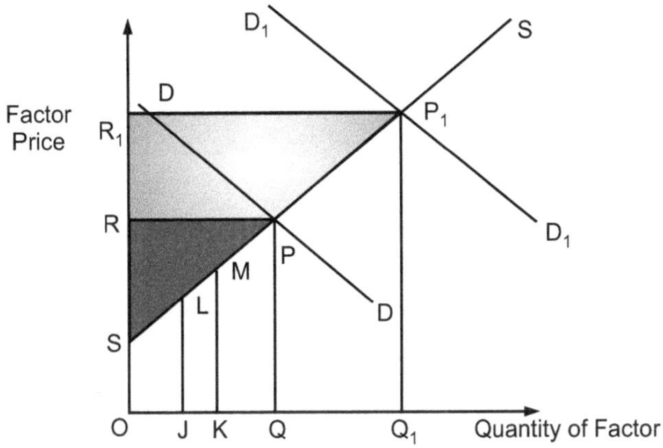

Fig. 4.11

In the above Fig. 4.11, if OJ units are supplied, LJ is the minimum supply price or TE and for OK units of supply, minimum supply price = MK. When DD is the demand interacting with upward sloping supply curve SS, OR is the factor price and total earnings are ORPQ. But TEs is measured by the area below the SS curve= OSPQ.

Therefore Economic Rent = ORPQ - OSPQ

= SRP

and if demand curve shifts to D_1D_1, factor price increases to OR_1,

total earnings = $OR_1\ P_1Q_1$

TEs = OSP_1Q_1

Economic Rent = $OR_1P_1Q_1 - OSP_1Q_1$

= SR_1P_1 (higher rent)

Therefore rent is determined on the basis of demand.

(iii) Consider the case of a factor having perfectly elastic supply

In this case, TEs are the same as actual earnings. Hence, the rent is zero. This can be depicted as follows:

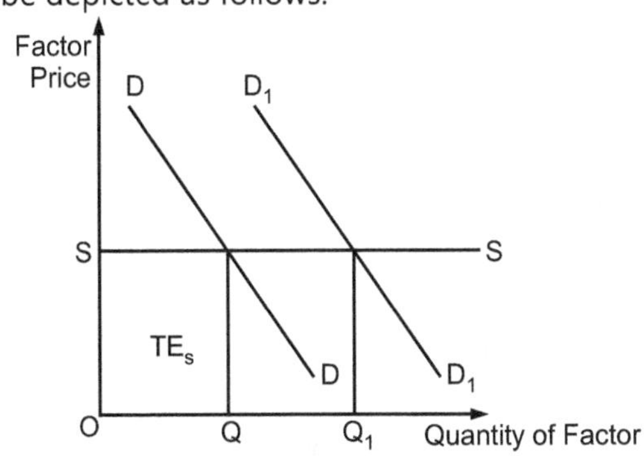

Fig. 4.12

In the above Fig. 4.12, even if demands shift to D_1D_1, supply is perfectly adjusted to the increase in demand at the same minimum supply price OS, so that the actual price also remains unchanged. Hence though the total earnings of the factor rises, the TEs also rise proportionately, with the increasing employment of the factor. So, rent as a surplus does not arise.

Therefore, according to the modern theory of rent:

(a) When the supply of the factor is **perfectly inelastic,** its **entire earnings** are **economic rent.**

(b) When the supply of the factor is **less than perfectly elastic,** its **total earnings** include a part of **economic rent**. Greater the degree of inelasticity, greater is the element of economic rent.

(c) When the **supply of the factor** is **perfectly elastic** its **entire earnings** are **equal to TEs.** Therefore there is **no element** of **economic rent.**

Hence a factor would earn economic rent only when its supply is less than perfectly elastic.

3. Quasi-Rent:

The idea of quasi-rent was introduced by Alfred Marshall. It refers to the short run earnings of some factors of production, which may be fixed in the short run but not in the long run. These factors of production include capital such as machines and other man-made instruments, factory buildings, ships etc. Unlike land, these factors of production are in fixed supply only in the short period, their supply is elastic in the long run.

In the short period, their supply is inelastic. Hence when demand rises, their income increases and they earn a surplus. This surplus is temporary because their supply becomes elastic in the long run. Therefore in the long run, when demand increases, supply increase and adjusts to the increase in demand. Hence these factors do not earn any surplus in the long run.

In a strict sense, the short run surplus earned from the use of these factors cannot be regarded as rent, although they look like rent due to its inelastic supply. Therefore Marshall calls it 'quasi rent' (meaning just like rent).

Thus quasi rent is a short term temporary surplus earning of some factors. It refers to the short term extra income earned by a factor in excess of its normal return. For example when there is a sudden increase in the demand for a particular kind of skilled labour, its supply cannot be increased immediately. Therefore the new increase in demand leads to a rise in the price of the skilled labour. This increase in price can be termed as quasi-rent. However, in the long run, the supply of this skilled labour can expand and consequently the supply increases to match the demand and the price comes down to its normal level. Therefore the surplus earning disappears. Hence, quasi-rent is a short run phenomenon.

Stonier and Hague have analysed quasi-rent and say that in the short run, any return earned by the use of a machine in excess of its variable costs can be regarded as quasi rent.

i.e. Quasi Rent = STR - STVC where

STR = Total Revenue in the short run.

STVC = Total variable costs in the short run.

This can be diagrammatically illustrated as follows:

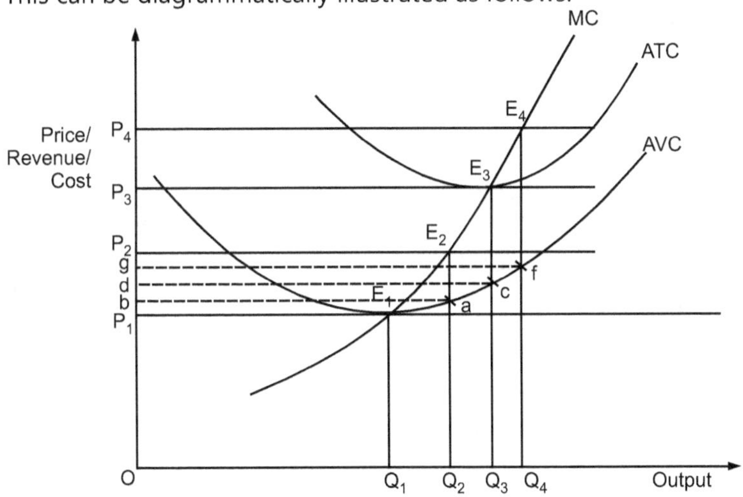

Fig. 4.13

In the above Fig. 4.13, it can be seen that the firm will continue to remain in business in the short run as long as it recovers its variable costs. Thus the minimum supply price of the firm's output is the short run TVC and any return in excess of this is a surplus i.e. quasi rent.

At price OP_1 equilibrium is at E_1 and output OQ_1.

$$TR = OP_1 E_1 Q_1;$$

$$TVC = TR$$

Hence, no surplus and no quasi-rent.

Any increase in demand leads to an increase in price to OP_2 at which OQ_2 is produced.

$$TR = OP_2 E_2 Q_2 \text{ and quasi-rent} = P_2 E_2 ab$$

Any further increase in demand leads to increase in price to OP_3 at which OQ_3 is produced.

$$TR = OP_3 E_3 Q_3 \text{ and quasi-rent} = P_3 E_3 cd$$

Any further increase in demand leads to increase in price to OP_4 at which OQ_4 is produced.

$$TR = OP_4 E_4 Q_4 \text{ and quasi rent} = P_4 E_4 fg$$

Quasi-rent is price determined and it is thus a short run phenomenon.

4.4 WAGES

4.4.1 Meaning and Types of Wages

The term 'wages' means, payments made for the services of labour. A wage payment is essentially a price paid for a particular commodity, namely labour services. There is no doubt that labour has peculiarities of its own which differentiate it from other commodities, yet like a commodity, labour is bought and sold. Labour participates in an exchange relationship i.e. the worker gives his time or labour and in exchange, gets money including some fringe benefits, if any.

Wages and Salary:

Economists make a small differentiation between wage and salary. Wage is the price of labour and salary as that of organisation. In accounting, however, the difference is made by making wages as direct expense and salary as indirect expense. **Wage** usually refers to payment to unskilled labour, while **salary** is a payment of skilled labour. Most labour markets are differentiated on the basis of the kinds of skills and training required in labour.

(a) Minimum Wages: A typical example of a price floor is the minimum wage. Minimum wage laws dictate the lowest price for labour that any employer may pay. The Minimum Wages Law ensures workers a minimally adequate standard of living.

To understand the effects of a minimum wage, we can consider the market for labour.

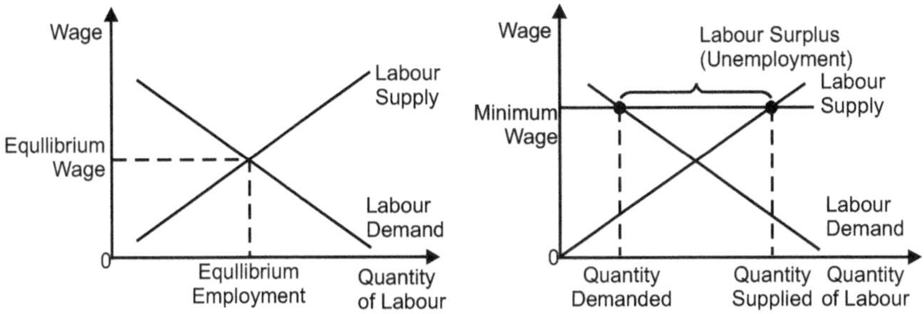

(a) A free labour market **(b) A labour market with a binding minimum wage**

Fig. 4.14: How minimum wage effects the labour market

Panel (a) of Fig. 4.14 shows the labour market, which like all markets is subject to the forces of demand and supply. Workers determine the supply of labour and firms determine the demand. If the Government does not intervene, the wage normally adjusts to balance labour supply and labour demand.

Panel (b) of Fig. 4.14 shows the labour market with a minimum wage. If the minimum wage is above the equilibrium level, the quantity of labour supplied exceeds the quantity demanded. This results in unemployment. Thus, the minimum wage raises the incomes of these workers who have jobs, but it lowers the incomes of workers who cannot find jobs.

However, it has to be kept in mind, that the economy contains not a single labour market but many labour market for different types of workers. The impact of the minimum wage depends on the skill and experience of the worker. Experienced workers with high skills are not affected because their equilibrium wages are well above the minimum. The minimum wage is not binding on such workers.

The minimum wages has its greatest impact on unskilled and least experienced labour. Their equilibrium wages are low. In addition to altering the quantity of such labour demanded, the minimum wage also alters the quantity supplied. Because the minimum wage raises the wage that such workers can earn, it increases the number of such workers who choose to look for jobs.

The minimum wage is often a topic of debate. Proponents of the minimum wage view the policy as one way to raise the income of the working poor. They correctly point out that workers who earn the minimum wage can afford only a meagre standard of living. Many of the proponents also admit that it has some adverse effects, including **unemployment**. However, they believe that these effects are small and that, all things considered, a higher minimum wage makes the poor better off.

Those opposing the minimum wage contend that it is not the best way to combat poverty. They are of the view that minimum wage causes unemployment - if there were no minimum wage laws, some workers who currently cannot find any firm willing to hire them at the minimum wage (as per law) would be able to find employment at a lower wage.

But at the same time it has to be kept in mind that those workers who still have jobs benefit from the minimum wage because they are paid a higher wage than they otherwise would be. In other words, minimum wage law creates both losers (workers who become unemployed and the firms have to pay higher wages) and winners (the workers who receive higher wages).

India introduced the Minimum Wages Act in 1948 and it has been amended from time to time.

(b) **Money wages** or **nominal wages** are the wages paid or received in terms of money per hour, per day, per week and so forth. But money wages alone may not give us a correct idea of what a worker really earns from his work. For this real wages have to be considered.

(c) **Real wages** are the quantity of goods and services which one can obtain with his money wages; real wages are the 'purchasing power' of money wages. In order to ascertain real wages, the following factors have to be taken into consideration:

(i) **Purchasing power of money:** The purchasing power of money varies inversely with price level; i.e. higher the prices lower the purchasing power of money and vice-versa.

(ii) **Subsidiary earnings:** In addition to the regular money wage, an employee has extra earnings in the form of money or goods. E.g. housing benefits, travelling allowance etc. This also adds to his purchasing power or real wages.

(iii) **Extra work without extra payment:** If an employee is required to do extra work without any compensation, his real wages are less by that extent.

(iv) **Regularity or irregularity of employment:** Regular or more secure employments may give lower money wages, but the real wages may be higher. On the other hand irregular and insecure employments may give high money wages but the real wages may be lower.

(v) **Conditions of work:** Some occupations are healthier than others and in some the hours of work are shorter than in others. All this has to be taken into account in estimating a person's real earnings.

(vi) **Future prospects:** A low money income will be considered a high real wage if there are good prospects of a rise in the future.

(d) **Subsistence Wages:** They are wages that provide only the bare necessities of life. It is the lowest wage upon which a worker and his or her family can survive.

The Subsistence Theories of Wages (originated in the Physiocratic School of France in the 18th Century) emphasize the supply side of the labour market. They hold that change in the supply of labour is the **main force** that derives real wages to the minimum required for subsistence (basic needs such as food, clothing and shelter to maintain existence).

Adam Smith referred to elements of the Subsistence Theory in his book, "The Wealth of Nations", where he held that the wages paid to workers had to be enough to allow them to live and to support their families.

Following Adam Smith, other classical economists such as David Ricardo and Thomas Malthus also held a similar outlook. Ricardo subscribed to the view that the "natural price" of labour was simply the price necessary to enable the labourers to subsist and to perpetuate the race. Ricardo's view was in tune with the Malthusian Theory of Population, which held that population adjusts to the means of supporting it.

Subsistence theorists argued that the market price of labour would not vary from the natural price for long - if wages rose above subsistence, the number of workers would increase and bring the wage rates down, if wages fell below subsistence, the number of workers would decrease and push the wage rates up. During the

18th Century, when these economists wrote, most workers were actually living near the subsistence level and population appeared to be trying to outpace the means of subsistence. Thus, the Subsistence Theory seemed to fit the facts. Later writers were much more pessimistic about the prospects for wage earners. Their inflexible conclusion that wages would always be driven down earned the Subsistence Theory, the name "Iron Law of Wages".

(e) Fair Wages: They are minimum wage rates for specific occupations. They must be paid by contractors doing work for Governments with fair wage policies. These policies, generally apply to construction, trades and sometimes cleaning and security workers and are often tied to union wage rates. They are intended to ensure contractors pay decent wages on government contracts instead of slashing wages and benefits.

A fair wage is something more than the minimum wages. Fair wage is a mean between the living wage and the minimum wage - (Living wage is a wage sufficient to ensure the workman and his family food, shelter, clothing, frugal comfort, provision for contingencies against ill-health, education for children and measures of insurance against old age). While the lower limit of the fair wage, is the minimum wage, the upper limit is the capacity of the industry to pay fair wage in reasonable comparison with the average payment of similar task in other trades or occupations requiring the same amount of ability. Fair wage depends on the present economic position as well as on future prospects. Thus fair wages depends upon the following factors:

(i) Minimum wages.

(ii) Capacity of industry to pay.

(iii) Prevailing rates of wages in the same or similar occupations in the same or neighbouring localities.

(iv) Productivity of labour.

(v) Level of national income and its distribution.

(vi) The place of the industry in the economy of the country.

Hence it is a wage that is reasonable for the type of work done. It is an adjustable step that moves up according to the capacity of the industry to pay and the prevailing wage rates in the area of industry.

4.4.2 Modern Theory of Wages

Although labour has certain peculiarities and cannot be regarded as an ordinary commodity, still wages are very largely determined by the interaction of the forces of demand and supply as in the case of an ordinary commodity.

Demand for labour: The demand for labour reflects partly labour's productivity and partly the market value of the product at different levels of production. The demand for labour is determined by:

(i) The nature of demand for the product of labour. Thus the demand for labour is a derived demand.

(ii) The proportion of the cost of labour to the total cost of the product.

(iii) Its substitutability by other factors.

(iv) Supply of capital as determined by the ability and willingness of investors to save and invest.

After considering all the above factors, the employer is governed by one fundamental factor, namely marginal productivity. The wages that he will pay to a labour (the marginal unit of labour) will be equal to the value of the additional product or marginal productivity. But since all the labour units are homogeneous, what is paid to the marginal worker will be paid to all the labourers.

The change in wage rate determines the direction of change in the demand for labour but the degree of this change depends on the elasticity of demand for labour. Whether the demand for labour is elastic or not will depend on: (a) the technical conditions of production and (b) elasticity of demand for the commodity which the labour produces. Generally, the short-term demand for labour is less elastic than the long-term demand. That is why the employers and the trade unions adopt a stiff attitude in wage negotiations.

It is important to remember that it is the demand of the entire industry, not of an individual firm, which determines wages in the market. The individual firm has to accept the market rate of wages and adjust its own demand for labour accordingly. The demand curve of the industry is derived from the lateral summation of the demand curves of individual firms.

Supply of Labour:

The supply of labour means the number of hours of a given type of labour which will be offered for hire at different wage rates. Usually, the relationship between the price of labour (wages) and the total amount of labour supplied in the market is a direct one i.e. a greater quantity of labour is offered at rising wage levels. Hence supply curve of labour slopes upwards from left to right.

The supply of labour depends on a number of factors like:

(a) The rate of population growth,

(b) The age and distribution of population, working hours,

(c) Labour laws regarding the employment of child and women labour,

(d) The attitude of labour in general towards work and leisure,

(e) The mobility of labour.

The mobility of labour determines the elasticity of supply of labour. If labour is mobile, its supply will be elastic i.e. a small rise in the wage rate of this type of labour will attract a large number of workers from other occupations and a small fall in the wage rate will lead to an outflow of workers to other occupations. If labour is less mobile between occupations, its supply will be inelastic i.e. a rise or a fall in wages can neither attract the workers into particular occupations, or drive the workers out of the occupations.

An important factor in the supply of labour is the **work-leisure ratio;** which in turn is affected by changes in wage rates. The effect of wage rates is of two types:

(i) Substitution effect

(ii) Income effect

When wage rate rises, it induces the worker to work more at the cost of leisure. Hence there is a **positive substitution effect** in favour of work.

But it is also true that workers prefer leisure to work when their income increases. Therefore, at higher wage rates they may be willing to work less than before. Here there is a **negative income effect** which discourages work and encourages leisure.

Therefore, when wage rate rises, there is a positive substitution effect and a negative income effect.

At lower wages rates, the positive substitution effect is greater than the negative income effect. Hence an increase in wage rate leads to an increase in supply of labour. But beyond a certain high level of wages, the negative income effect is greater than the positive substitution effect. Therefore an increase in wage rate leads to a fall in supply of labour.

Accordingly the **supply curve of labour** is not upward sloping throughout its length but is **backward sloping** showing that beyond a certain wage level, the workers' preference for leisure becomes more dominant against their will to work. This can be illustrated as follows:

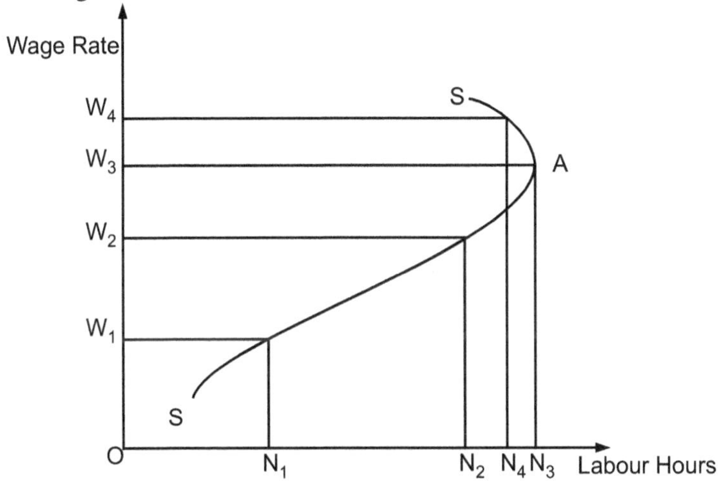

Fig. 4.15

In the above Fig. 4.15, it is clear that SS is the backward bending supply curve of labour which bends backwards at point A. As wage rate rises from OW_1 to OW_2 to OW_3 the supply of labour rises from ON_1 to ON_2 to ON_3. However any further rise in wage to say OW_4 brings about a fall in supply of labour to ON_4.

Interaction of Demand and Supply: The interaction of demand and supply of labour determines the wage level. This is shown in Fig. 4.16 (a) and 4.16 (b).

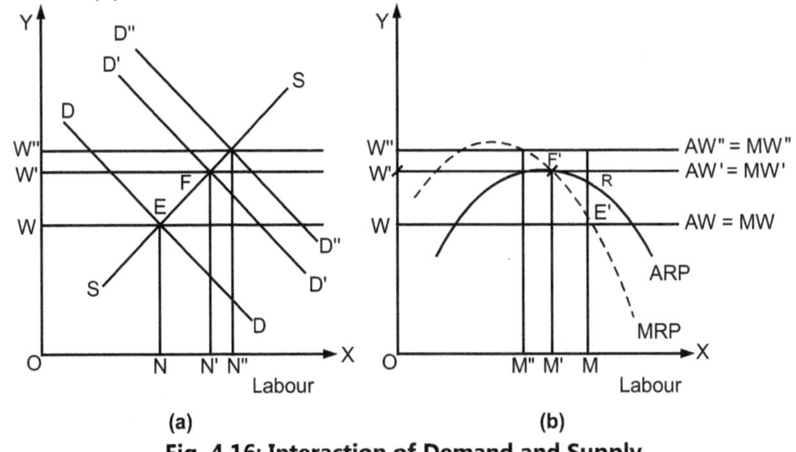

Fig. 4.16: Interaction of Demand and Supply

In Fig. 4.16 (a) we take the case of an industry. The curve SS represents supply to the industry. DD is the demand curve. They intersect at E. The wage level, therefore, is OW (= EN).

Fig. 4.16 (b) represents the case of a firm. Under perfect competition, the firm has to accept the market wage OW settled by the industry above. From the OW level in Fig. 4.16 (a) draw a straight line towards Fig. 4.16 (b) representing the condition of the firm. The extended line W-AW cuts the MRP curve of the firm at E′ in Fig. 4.16 (b). But at this level, the ARP is MR which is greater than the wage OW. Hence all the firms are making supernormal profits at this wage level. This will lead to entry of new firms in the industry; the demand for labour will increase and the wage level will go up. Thus, the SNP will be competed away in the long run by the entry of new firms.

The new demand curve D′D′ cuts the supply curve SS in Fig. 4.16 (a) at F. The wage level in this situation will be OW′ which is higher than the original wage level OW. This is how the interaction of demand and supply determines the wage. When the wage is OW, the firm is in equilibrium at E′ and when the wage rises to OW′, the equilibrium is at F′. At this point, ARP and MRP are equal and the average wage OW′ is equal to both of them.

It can also happen that the occurrence of SNPs attracts some firms from outside, which may further increase the demand for labour to D″D″. The wage level will then be OW″. Here the ARP is less than the wage OW″, i.e. the firms are suffering losses. The result will be that some firms will leave the industry, and the wage will come down to the level of OW′. Here, the wage, ARP and MRP are all equal.

Thus, under perfect competitive conditions, wages are, in the long run equal to MRP as well as ARP of labour.

Exploitation of Labour

It is a well known fact that labour has a weak bargaining power in relation to the employer; hence exploitation of labour. As defined by Joan Robinson, labour is said to be exploited when the wage is less than the value of the marginal product (VMP), which is equal to the physical product multiplied by the sale price of the product. There can be no exploitation of labour under perfect competition both in the labour market and in the product market. In this case, price and MR are equal (VMP=MRP) and labour is paid the wage rate equal to the value of its marginal product.

But in other market situations, labour exploitation occurs. There are three types of exploitation

Monopsonistic Exploitation: When an industrial employer or a group of employers occupy a very strong monopolistic position as compared with labour, it constitutes what is called monopsony. In monopsony, the employer embodies in his person, concentrated monopoly power of being the sole purchaser of labour, whereas labour occupies a very weak position in comparison. Monopsony also occurs when a big employer employs proportionately a very large number of a given type of labour so that he is in a position to influence the wage rate. It may also occur when a group of big employers come to an understanding not to compete for labour and thus act as a single hirer of labour. In this situation, each worker gets a wage less than MRP. This is the measure of labour exploitation under monopsony. This is called monopsonistic exploitation, (Mrs. Joan Robinson).

Monopolistic Exploitation: In this case, there is perfect competition in the labour market (average and marginal wage curves coincide) but imperfect competition in the product market, i.e. MR is less than the price of the product and therefore the MRP is less than the value of the marginal product (VMP). In equilibrium, the firm will equate their wages with MRP. This means that labour is paid less than the value of the marginal product which shows exploitation.

Double Exploitation: It occurs when there is imperfect competition both in the labour market (monopsony) and in the product market (monopoly). Thus there is double exploitation of labour both monopsonistic and monopolistic and labour is exploited the most.

4.4.3 Collective Bargaining

One of the many purposes of the theory of wages is to analyse the effect of collective bargaining on wages. In modern labour economics collective bargaining has assumed a pride of place. Worker's nowadays, combine and form a trade union to press collectively on their employer for higher wages. Many times such pressure becomes effective but in certain circumstances it proves harmful to the workers. Whether a demand for higher wages through collective bargaining would be acceded to by the employer or not depends upon the conditions prevailing in the factor market and the product market.

Conceptually, the following four circumstances of collective bargaining may arise

(It is *assumed throughout the analysis of collective bargaining that the trade union will demand a higher but equal wage to each of its* member).

When both the product market and the labour market, are perfectly competitive: In the circumstance where trade union demand a higher but equal wage to each of its member, the trade union would not be benefited pressurizing on the employers. This is because; higher wages are associated with some degree of unemployment.

When the product market is monopolistic and the labour market is monopsonistic: This means that the buyer of the labour as well as the seller of the product is one firm only. Since the firm is monopolistic its demand curve or (MRP) curve would be steeper and at the same time the supply curve of labour (MW) would be rising upwards because it is monopsonistic.Thus a pressure on the entrepreneurs by his labourers for raising wages by means of collective bargaining will be favourably responded to by the firm. There will be twofold benefit in this process. One, the wage would be raised and the other, more workers would be employed i.e. the firm would need more workers to maximize its profits.

When the product market is perfectly competitive but the labour market is monopsonistic: This type of situation yields similar results as the monopolistic and monopsonistic situation. In other words the workers will be successful to obtain higher wages subject to the maximum equal to their MRP. In case the worker's organisation is unwise enough to press for wages higher than MRP it will have to face unemployment.

When the product market is monopsonistic but the labour market is perfectly competitive: Here collective bargaining is hard to get higher wages without some amount of unemployment. Of course, the workers who are being paid somewhat less than their marginal revenue productivities will now be able to earn wages equivalent to their marginal revenue productivities. Wages with no unemployment can increase only if MRP increases so as to offset the likely unemployment.

Trade Unions and Wage Determination

Establishment of a strong trade union introduces an element of monopoly in the labour market. Instead of each worker negotiating with the employer on the question of wages, the trade union bargains on behalf of them all. For a long time, economists held the view that the trade union action in increasing wages was futile and ineffective. The classical economists argued that wages could be raised only at the expense of profits and a fall in profits, by reducing industrial activity, would reduce demand for labour and cause unemployment.

But modern economists do not subscribe to the above view. They strongly hold that trade unions can raise wages in a number of ways:

(i) Stopping Exploitation: The trade unions can ensure that labour is paid the full value of its marginal productivity. Competition in the real world is not perfect. Hence, wages do not come up to the marginal productivity level due to the weak bargaining power of labour. By improving their bargaining power, the trade unions can raise wages up to the marginal productivity level and put an end to the exploitation of labour by powerful employers.

(ii) Raising Marginal Productivity: Trade unions can improve the marginal productivity of labour itself: (a) They can force the employer to use more up-to-date appliances and organisation (b) They improve the efficiency of labour itself. (c) Trade unions may also increase the marginal productivity of a particular group of labourers by restricting its supply.

(iii) Restricting Labour Supply: The trade unions usually adopt a number of restrictive devices eg. forcing the government to pass immigration laws, pressing for the reduction of working hours, restricting entry to the union and not permitting non-union labour to work etc. The aim clearly is to raise wages by reducing supply of labour when demand for it remains the same. There are special circumstances in which a particular set of workers can raise their wages by withdrawing their supply: (a) when the demand for the group of labour is inelastic, (b) when the wages of the said group form a small proportion of the total cost of production of the commodity concerned, and (c) when the other factors of production are "squeezable".

(iv) Raising Standard Wage Rates: Instead of putting restrictions on the supply of labour, modern trade unions fight for the raising of standard wage rates. Once certain wage rates are accepted by a representative body of the industry, individual firms quickly fall in line.

(v) Increasing Labour Demand: The trade unions also adopt ways and means to increase the demand for labour on the part of the employers:

The unions try to shift the derived demand curve upward. For instance, by improving labour productivity, they may enable the management to reduce the cost of production and hence the price. This in turn will increase the demand.

The unions may agitate for the protection of the industry so that domestic industry expands and employs more labour.

They may influence the government to pay higher rates on public contracts for the goods made by the industry.

They may help the employers to charge a high monopoly price and wrest a share for labour out of monopoly profits.

Some unions have agitated for higher tariff in order to increase the domestic demand for goods they produce and consequently for labour used in their production.

(vi) **The trade unions can raise wages, because a large part of this rise can come about by squeezing the rent** element in the factors of production and monopoly gains in other incomes.

(vii) Lastly, the raising of wages by the unions will not necessarily discourage investment. Today the bulk of investment comes not from individuals but from big corporations which usually maintain the level of investment but reduce dividend to shareholders when their income falls.

4.5 INTEREST

Meaning: Interest has been the most controversial topic in the whole theory of distribution. Economists have differed regarding the nature of interest as well as how it is determined. Interest is a payment for the use of capital. According to Marshall interest is "the price paid for the use of capital in any market." Interest is expressed as a percentage return on capital invested after allowing for risks of investment.

Net Interest and Gross Interest

Net Interest is a reward paid to capitalists for the use of capital only. In other words, net interest is the payment made purely for the use of capital. Marshall defined net interest as the earning of capital simply as the reward for waiting. Our analysis is concerned with net interest or pure interest only.

Gross interest is the amount paid by a borrower to a lender as a return on capital borrowed. Gross interest includes some charges other than the net interest. Besides the price for the use of capital, gross interest also includes reward for risk of lending money, return for inconvenience, return for management of loan etc. Gross interest consists of the following components:

(i) Net interest: this includes the price for the use of capital alone.

(ii) Reward for risk-taking: When interest is charges, besides the price for the use of capital, the lender also includes the return for taking risk. If risk is more, rate of interest will be higher than the price for the use of capital and vice-versa.

(iii) Reward for management: A lender has to keep all the accounts of his lending business. The expenditure that he incurs on managing the accounts is added to the interest that he charges from the borrower.

(iv) Reward for inconveniences: When a lender charges interest he includes in it the price of all the inconveniences involved in recovery of the loans.

Therefore, **Gross Interest = *Net Interest + Return for risk + Return for inconvenience + Return for*** management ***of loan.***

Concept of capital, saving and investment

To understand the concepts of capital, saving and investment it would be appropriate to study the **Classical** or **Real Theory of Interest** which seeks to explain the determination of the rate of interest by real factors i.e. productivity of capital goods and saving of goods. According to this theory, rate of interest is determined by the demand for savings to invest in capital goods and the supply of savings.

Demand for savings: The demand for capital goods comes from firms which desire to invest i.e. to purchase or to make new capital goods. Capital goods are demanded because they can be used to produce consumer goods: because they have revenue productivity like all other factors. For any given type of capital asset, e.g. a machine, it is possible to draw a marginal revenue productivity curve showing the addition made to the total revenue by an additional unit of a machine at various levels of the stock of that machine.

But the marginal revenue productivity of capital is a more complex concept than that of other factors. The entrepreneurs have to take into consideration the uncertainties of the future and estimate the percentage yield or returns from capital after making allowance for maintenance and operating costs. i.e. they have to find out the **net expected return** of a marginal unit of capital expressed as percentage of the cost of the capital asset. The more capital assets of a given kind an entrepreneur has, the less revenue or income he will expect to earn by purchasing one more machine of the same kind. Therefore the marginal revenue productivity curve of capital slopes downwards towards the right as shown below.

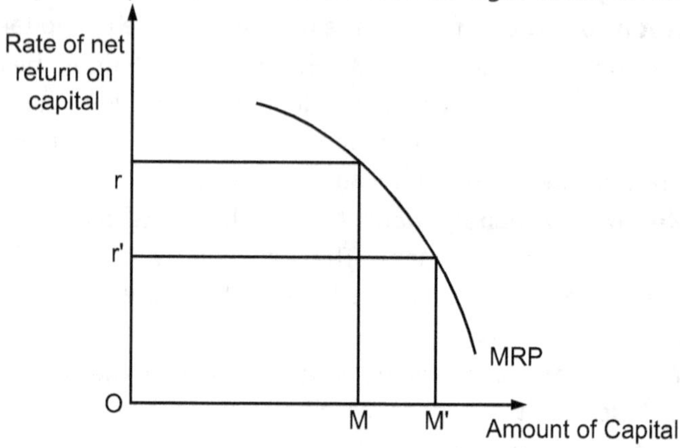

Fig. 4.17

In the above Fig. 4.17, at Or rate of interest, OM amount of capital is demanded. This is so because only at OM amount of capital, the falling net rate of return on capital becomes equal to the prevailing rate of interest Or. If rate of interest falls from Or to Or′, the amount of capital demanded will increase from OM to OM′ Thus the MRP curve of capital shows the **demand for capital** (or demand for savings to buy the capital) which slopes downwards towards the right. This is true of individual firms, industries and of the community as a whole. Thus demand for capital goods will increase as rate of interest falls.

Supply of savings: The money which is to be used for purchasing capital goods is made available by those who save from their current income. By postponing consumption of a part of their current income, they release resources for productive purposes. Savings involve the element of waiting for the future enjoyment of savings. More savings the people do the more consumption they will have to postpone. Thus to induce people to save more, higher rates of interest must be offered. Hence supply curve of capital will slope upwards to the right.

Equilibrium between Demand and Supply

The rate of interest is determined by the interaction of the forces of demand for capital (or investment) and the supply of savings. This is illustrated as follows:

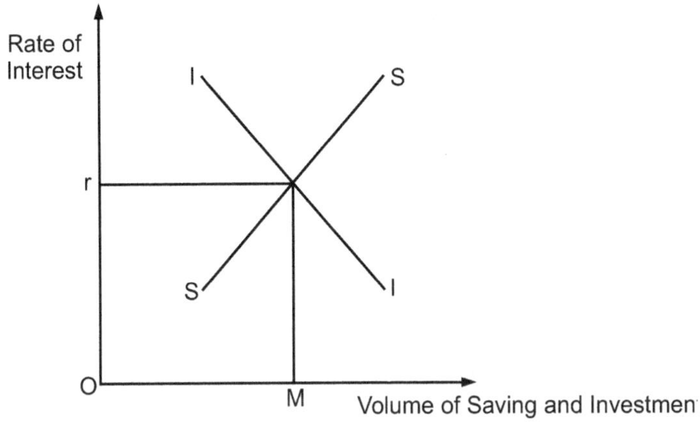

Fig. 4.18

In the above Fig. 4.18, SS is the supply curve of savings and II is the demand curve of savings to invest in capital goods. The two curves intersect each other at Or rate of interest when OM amount of money is lent, borrowed and invested.

Loanable Funds Theory of Interest

This is also called the Neo-Classical Theory of Interest. It asserts that rate of interest is determined by the equilibrium between demand and supply of loanable funds in the credit market. Hence interest is the price paid for the use of loanable funds.

Supply of Loanable Funds: This is derived from 4 basic sources:

- **(a) Savings (S):** Savings by individuals or households constitute the most important source of loanable funds. Savings are looked at in either of the two ways:
  - (i) As **ex-ante savings** i.e. savings planned by individuals at the beginning of a period in the hope of expected incomes and anticipated expenditures on consumption.
  - (ii) Savings as the difference between the income of the preceding period and the consumption of the present period. Savings primarily depend upon the size of incomes. But given the level of income, savings vary at various rates of interest.
- **(b) Dishoarding (DH):** Individuals may dishoard money from the hoarded stock of the previous period. Thus cash balances, lying idle in a previous period, become active balances in the present period. At higher rates of interests more will be dishoarded.

(c) **Bank Credit (BM):** Banks by creating money can advance loans to businessmen. This adds to the supply of loan funds. Banks can also reduce the amount of money by contracting their lending. Generally speaking, banks will lend more money at higher rates of interest than at lower ones, other things remaining the same.

(d) **Disinvestment (DI):** This is the opposite of investment and takes place when due to structural changes or bad venture, the existing stock of machines and other equipment is allowed to wear out without being replaced or when inventories are drawn below the level of the previous period. Disinvestment is encouraged by a high rate of interest on loanable funds.

The lateral summation of the savings, dishoarding, disinvestment and bank credit results in a total supply curve of loanable funds (LS) which slopes upwards to the right showing that a greater amount of loanable funds will be available at higher rates of interest and vice versa. (Refer Fig. 4.19)

Demand for Loanable Funds: This comes from three fields:

(a) **Investment (I):** The bulk of demand for loanable funds comes from business firms which borrow money for purchasing or making new capital goods, including the building up of inventories. The price of the loanable funds required to purchase the capital goods is the rate of interest. The demand for loanable funds for investment purposes is interest elastic and slopes downward to the right.

(b) **Consumption (C):** Demand for loanable funds comes from individual or households who want to borrow for consumption purposes. Loans for consumption are demanded for buying durable goods like automobiles, refrigerators etc. Demand for loanable funds for consumption purposes is interest elastic and slopes downward to the right.

(c) **Hoarding (I):** Demand for loanable funds may come from those who want to hoard money: to hold savings as idle cash balances. The demand for hoarding money is interest elastic and slopes downward to the right. At higher rates of interest, people will hoard or hold less money and vice versa. (Refer Fig. 4.19)

Equilibrium between demand for and supply of Loanable Funds

The rate of interest will be determined by the equilibrium between the total demand for loanable funds and total supply of loanable funds. This is illustrated as follows:

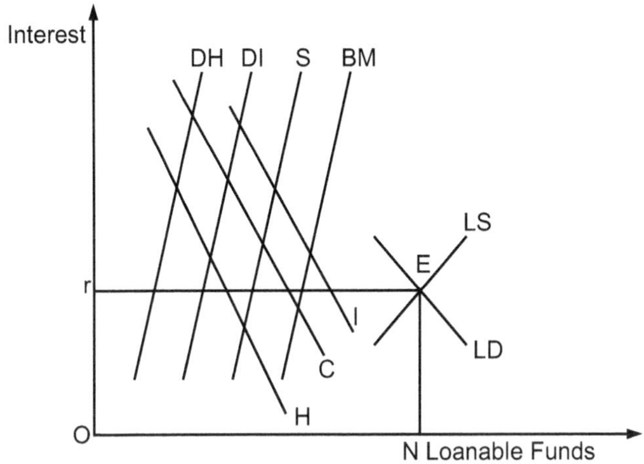

Fig. 4.19

In the above Fig. 4.19, LS is the total supply curve of loanable funds derived by the lateral summation of dishoarding (DH), disinvestment (DI), savings (S) and bank credit (BM). Total demand curve for loanable funds is LD derived by the lateral addition of hoarding (H), consumption (C) and investment (I). LD and LS intersect at rate of interest or where ON amount of loanable funds is borrowed (demanded) and lent (supplied).

Liquidity Preference Theory of Interest

This is one of the most important theories of interest advocated by **J. M. Keynes** in his book 'The General Theory of Employment, Interest and Money'. He defines the rate of interest as the reward for parting with liquidity during a specified period. It is the price which equates the desire to hold wealth in the form of cash with the available quantity of cash. In other words the rate of interest in the Keynesian sense is determined by the demand for and supply of money.

Demand for money: Keynes called the demand for money as 'Liquidity preference'. This refers to the desire to hold cash. According to Keynes, the desire for liquidity arises out of 3 motives:

(a) Transactions motive: This relates to the need for cash for current transactions i.e. for day to day requirements. The need for holding cash to meet the day to day requirements arises because of the interval between the receipts of income and expenditure i.e. income is received at the beginning of the month, while expenditure is spread out over the month. Hence the need for liquidity arises to bridge this gap between income and expenditure. The amount of liquid cash held for transactions is mainly dependent upon the level of income. The amount of money held under transactions motive is denoted by the letter M_1.

(b) Precautionary motive: This refers to the desire of the people to hold cash balances to meet unforeseen contingencies. i.e. both individuals and businessmen keep cash in reserve to meet unexpected needs such as illness, accidents, unemployment etc. The amount of money held under this motive will also depend upon the level of income. It is also conditioned by the nature of the individual and his view of life. Money held under precautionary motive is denoted by the letter M_2. Therefore the amount of money held under transactions motive (M_1) and under precautionary motive (M_2) depends upon the level of income (Y).

$$M_1 + M_2 = f(Y)$$

(c) Speculative motive: Money held under the speculative motive is for securing profit by taking advantage of changes in bond prices and rate of interest. Individuals and businessmen having surplus funds, after keeping enough for transactions and precautionary motives, like to gain by investing in bonds-buying at low prices and selling at high prices. The amount of money held under the speculative motive depends on the rate of interest. Bond prices and the rate of interest are inversely related to each other. [A bond carries a fixed rate of interest. Suppose, for instance, a bond of the value of ₹ 100 carries 4% interest. If the market rate of interest rises to 5%, the demand for this bond falls in the market with a consequent fall in price. On the other hand, if the market rate of interest falls to 3%, the demand for this bond rises with a consequent rise in its price.) Low bond prices are indicative of high interest rates and high bond prices reflect low interest rates. Thus, the speculative demand for money will be less at a high rate of interest because high rate of interest reflect low bond prices and it is possible that some of the businessmen convert their cash into bonds leaving less liquidity in their hands. On the other hand, if the interest rate is low, reflecting high bond prices, businessmen sell their bonds with the result that the liquidity in their hands is high. Therefore higher the rate of interest, lower is the speculative demand for money and lower the rate of interest, higher is the speculative demand for money. The speculative demand for money is denoted by the letter M_3. Since M_3 depends upon the rate of interest (r) or bond prices, the speculative demand function is written as $M_3 = f(r)$.

If the total demand for money (liquidity) is denoted by M then

$$M = M_1 + M_2 + M_3$$
$$M_1 + M_2 = f(Y)$$
$$M_3 = f(r)$$
$$M = f(Y,r)$$

The speculative demand for money can be illustrated as follows:

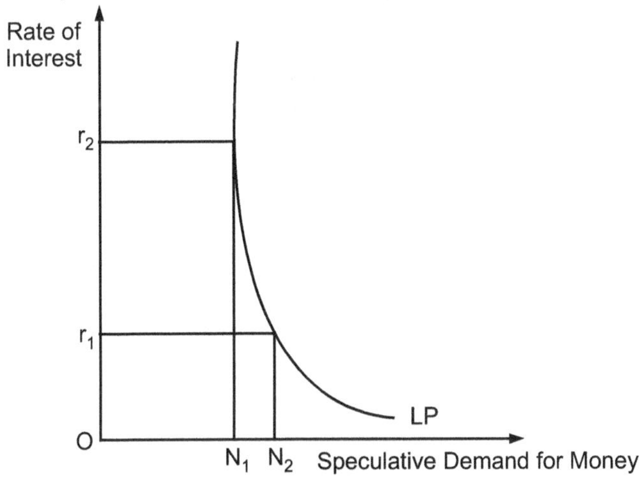

Fig. 4.20

In the above Fig. 4.20, LP indicates the (liquidity preference for speculation) speculative demand for money. At interest rate Or_2, the speculative demand for money is as small as ON_1 and at a lower interest rate of Or_1 speculative demand for money extends to ON_2. Keynes holds that the speculative demand curve becomes perfectly elastic at a certain low rate of interest. At this low rate of interest people prefer to keep money in cash. This position of the liquidity preference curve is called the **'Liquidity Trap'.**

Supply of money: This refers to the total quantity of money in a country for all purposes at any time. According to Keynes the supply of money is fixed by the monetary authorities. i.e. the supply curve of money is taken to be perfectly inelastic. This is depicted as follows:

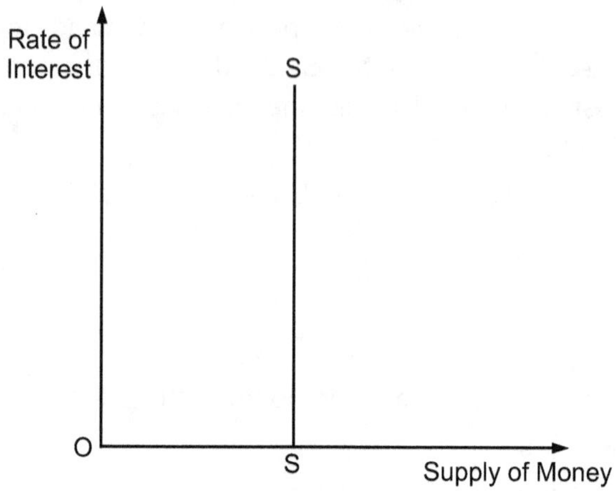

Fig. 4.21

In the above Fig. 4.21, SS is the perfectly inelastic supply curve of money.

Determination of the rate of interest

The rate of interest like the price of any product or service is determined by the demand (liquidity preference) and supply of money. In fact it is the liquidity preference for speculative motive along with the quantity of money that determines the rate of interest. This is depicted as follows:

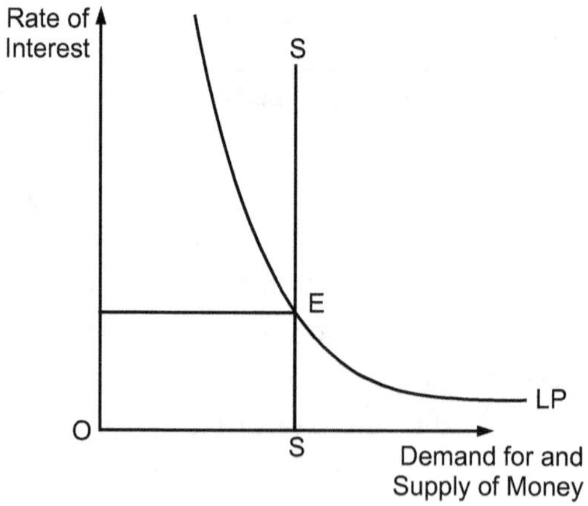

Fig. 4.22

In the above Fig. 4.22, SS indicates the inelastic supply curve of money and the curve LP indicates the liquidity preference for speculative motive. They intersect at E and the equilibrium rate of interest Or is determined. At this rate of interest the demand for money equals supply of money (OS).

Changes in demand for money: With supply remaining constant, any change in the liquidity preference tends to alter the rate of interest. When the liquidity preference curve shifts to the **right or upwards,** from LP_1 to LP_2 (because of an increase in the level of income), the rate of interest rises from Or_1 to Or_2. This is illustrated as follows:

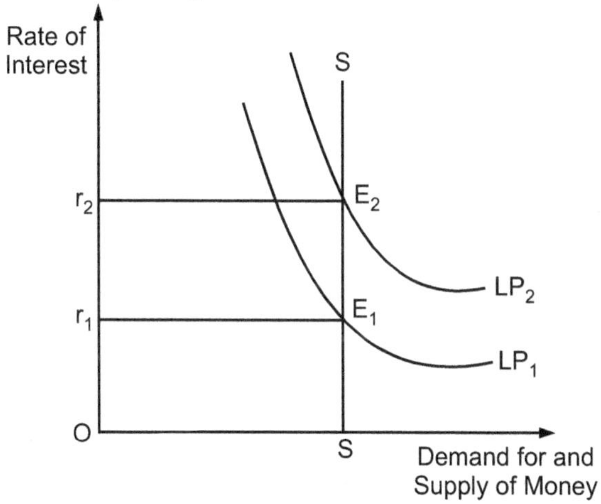

Fig. 4.23

In the above Fig. 4.23, the equilibrium point shifts from E_1 to E_2.

Changes in supply of money: With liquidity preference of the consumers remaining constant, an increase in the supply of money by the monetary authorities from S_1S_1 to S_2S_2 leads to a decline in the rate of interest from Or_1 or Or_2. This is illustrated as follows:

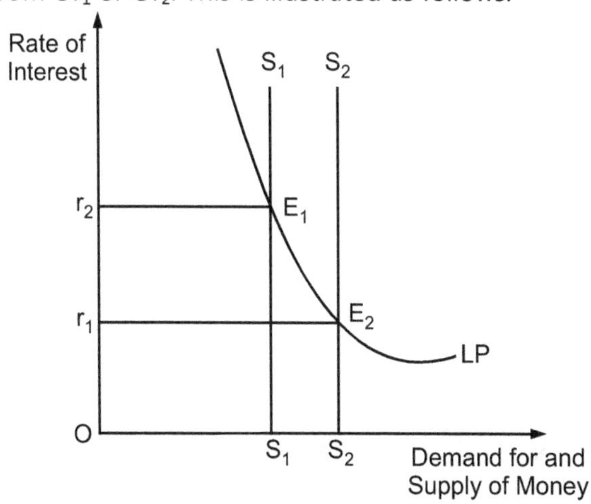

Fig. 4.24

In the above Fig. 4.24, the equilibrium points shifts from E_1 to E_2. Thus in the Keynesian theory of interest, interest is a purely monetary phenomenon determined by the demand for money and supply of money.

4.6 PROFIT

Meaning: Profit is the reward to the entrepreneur for his entrepreneurial functions. Among the four factors of production the entrepreneur occupies a unique place. He is unique in the sense that unlike other factors of production, he cannot be hired, for if he is hired he becomes a part of labour. It is this quality which keeps his position strategic in the mechanism of production.

Profit as a Residual Income:

Profits are ***residual income*** left after the payment of the contractual rewards to other factors of production. While employing factors of production, the entrepreneur enters into a contract with them: he pays rent on the land used, wages to workers employed and interest (at rates fixed by the contract) on the loans taken. Actually, the entrepreneur makes payment to these factors of production even before he has realized the value of the product produced through sale of the product. The profits of the entrepreneur is nothing but what is left after paying the contractual rewards to the factors of production. Thus profits are **non-contractual income** and therefore they may be positive or negative, whereas **contractual income** of other factors of production such as rent, wages and interest are always positive and are never negative. Profit differs from the return on other factors in three important respects:

(i) Profit is a **residual income** and not contractual or certain income as in the case of other factors.

(ii) There are much **greater fluctuations** in profits than in the rewards of the other factors.

(iii) Profits may be **negative** (loss) when $TR < TC$ whereas rent, wages and interest must always be positive.

In the **accounting sense** profit is TR - TC. But TC includes only explicit costs: contractual payments like wages, rent, interest, raw material cost, cost on fuel, depreciation charges etc.

In **economics** also profit is TR - TC. But this TC includes explicit as well as implicit costs such as imputed cost of a firm's own capital, land, entrepreneur's salary for his managerial skill. Profit is a surplus of firm's TR over TC (which includes explicit and implicit costs.) Profit is a return for the entrepreneurial ability. Normal profit is a part of cost of production. Therefore in economics normal profit is not true profit.

Economic profit is TR -TC (explicit and implicit cost including normal profit). Further as mentioned above, profit being a residual income can be negative (loss).

Gross Profit and Net Profit:

Gross Profit stands for the total earnings of the entrepreneur, not necessarily for the entrepreneurial functions only. It is composed of the following elements:

(i) Imputed cost of maintenance or depreciation charges.

(ii) Land, labour and capital may be owned and supplied by the entrepreneur himself. Hence the implicit rent, implicit wages and implicit interests are included in gross profit.

(iii) The imputed minimum return for the entrepreneur's organisational function - i.e. the return for the work done by the entrepreneur as manager and could have been done by him on a salary basis for another firm are also called normal profits and is included in gross profit.

(iv) Monopoly gains which are due to imperfect competition also form part of gross profits.

(v) Conjectural gains also called 'windfall gains' which may be due to favourable circumstances or pure luck also form part of gross profits.

(vi) Net profit or pure economic profit earned by the entrepreneur for his function of risk-taker - both insurable and non-insurable - and efficiency form part of gross profits.

Net Profit or Pure Profit:

Net profit is the income from risk-taking, it is a payment made exclusively for bearing risk. This essential function of the entrepreneur cannot be the task of management. It is the entrepreneur who assumes the final responsibility that cannot be shifted on to anyone else. Thus net profit is gross profit minus the first five elements of gross profit mentioned above such as imputed cost of maintenance or depreciation charges; implicit rent, implicit wages, implicit interest; normal profits; monopoly gains and conjectural gains.

Theories of Profit

(a) The Risk Bearing Theory of Profits

The risk-bearing theory of profits is associated with **F. B. Hawley.** According to him all businesses are more or less speculative and unless the risk-taker is amply rewarded, business will not be started. The greater the risk the higher must be the expected profit in order to induce people to start business. If there is no hope for substantial profit, no one will be willing to risk money by investing it in business. Hawley explained four types of risks which are undertaken by the entrepreneur:

(i) **Replacement** is also called depreciation. It can be calculated. It is added into the costs.

(ii) **Obsolescence** is not measurable because it is not always possible to anticipate technical progress.

(iii) **Risk proper** is the risk of marketability of the product.

(iv) **Uncertainty** is with regard to unforeseen factors.

(v) **Entrepreneurs** bear all these risks in the hope of earning profits. Hence profits can be called as 'costs of staying in businesses.

Criticism:

(i) This theory has been criticised on the ground that though profits do contain some remuneration for risk-taking, yet the high profits made by entrepreneurs cannot in their entirety be attributed to the element of risk. Profit is a mixed income. They arise not only due to risk-taking but also from the ability, managerial and bargaining powers of the entrepreneur.

(ii) Some critics point out that profits arise not because risks are borne by the entrepreneurs but because the superior entrepreneurs are able to reduce them.

(iii) Prof Knight pointed out that profits arise not due to all risks. Some risks can be foreseen and they can be insured and hence they can be covered. Profits occur due to only those risks which are unforeseen, unpredictable and not insurable.

(iv) It is wrong to believe that there is a proportionate relationship between risks and profits as was believed by Hawley. In reality, risks and profits are not rigidly related to each other.

Thus Hawley's risk-bearing theory of profits is incomplete.

(b) Prof Knight's Uncertainty-Bearing Theory of Profits

Prof. F.H. Knight made an improvement over the **risk bearing theory** and presented a refined version called the **'Uncertainty Bearing Theory of Profits'.** He has attributed the origin of profits to risks and uncertainty bearing. According to him risks are of 2 kinds.

(i) Risks that **can be insured** i.e. risks which are measurable and whose probability can be statistically measured. The risks of fire, theft and accidents are insurable and they are usually borne by the insurance companies. Hence insurable risks are not the real risks attributed to entrepreneurial functions.

(ii) **Risks that cannot be insured against** - There are certain risks which are incalculable and whose probability cannot be computed because of the presence of uncertainty. Such unforeseen risks relate to changes in prices, demand, supply etc. No insurance company can calculate the loss expected from such risks and hence they are non-insurable. These risks have to be borne by the entrepreneur himself. According to Prof. Knight Profit is the reward for bearing non-insurable risks or uncertainties. The uncertainties of business which are non-insurable include:

(a) Demand fluctuations which can occur due to change in income, tastes and fashions.
(b) Technological changes take place very rapidly.
(c) Changes in Government policies.
(d) Cyclical fluctuations.
(e) Political instability.
(f) Secular changes in the form of unforeseen changes in income, taste, size and composition of population etc.

Whenever a new product comes into the market, the entrepreneur has to decide whether the product will be approved by the consumers, whether the price is high or low and he has to determine the advertisement outlay. If his calculations and judgements are correct they make profits and if they go wrong they incur losses. Therefore according to Knight it is the non-insurable risks that involve uncertainty and give rise to profits.

Criticism:

(i) Uncertainty is not the only factor that limits the supply of entrepreneurs. Lack of funds, lack of knowledge, lack of opportunities and the presence of economic friction are some of the other factor that restrict the supply of entrepreneurs.
(ii) Uncertainty bearing is not the only function of the entrepreneur. The profit that he gets is also the reward for other services that he renders, e.g., initiating, co-ordinating etc.
(iii) Uncertainty-bearing cannot be elevated to the status of a factor of production. It is an element of real costs which means exertion, abstinence, sacrifice etc. as distinguished from money cost. Cost is not generally measured in terms of real cost. We know that capital is a factor of production, but abstinence is also needed to have capital.
(iv) Knight's theory does not have much relevance to the real world. Businessmen continue to estimate profits **ex-ante** in defiance of this theory.
(v) In modern times, the entrepreneurial function is divided among shareholders, directors and managers of the company. It is not clear in this theory as to who bears uncertainty.

Thus Knight's uncertainty-bearing theory of profits has been criticized as heavily insulated from empirical testing and empirical relevance.

(c) Dynamic Theory of Profits

This theory is associated with the name of the American economist **J. B. Clark.** Profits arise as a result of dynamic changes in the economy. According to Clark, profit is the difference between selling price and costs which emerges because of changes in demand and supply conditions.

In a static world (stationary conditions of demand and supply) where the size of population, amount of capital, the quantity and quality of human wants, the methods of production, technical knowledge, the organisation of business etc. remain constant, there is no real or pure profit. Hence under competitive conditions price equals AC and there is no surplus and no pure profit. Wherever there is a temporary surplus, production will increase, bringing down the price and the surplus disappears.

But the real world is a dynamic world, where changes are constantly taking place. There are **internal** changes which the entrepreneur himself brings about such as innovations, technological improvements, changes in the form of business organisation and **external** changes such as changes in tastes and preferences, increase in population etc. These changes make the economy dynamic and bring about changes in demand and supply conditions. Some entrepreneurs attain advantageous business positions and reap a surplus over costs and earn profits. Thus efficient entrepreneurs get profits while inefficient entrepreneurs who fail to keep pace with the dynamic changes do not earn any profit and may even incur a loss.

Criticism:

(i) The theory explains the difference between profits and wages. But it does not distinguish between the wages of an entrepreneur and his profits.

(ii) It fails to determine the size of profits.

(iii) The theory ignores profit as a reward for risk-taking. Risk-element cannot be ignored while determining profits.

(iv) The theory gives an inadequate explanation of the dynamic society. It explains only a few components of a dynamic society.

(v) It is incorrect to say that profits arise only due to the changes occurring in society. Profit is also earned due to the ability, organisational and managerial skill of the entrepreneur. Thus the dynamic theory of profits provides a poor explanation of the origin and nature of profits.

(d) The Innovation Theory of Profits

This theory was put forth by **Joseph Schumpeter.** According to him the main function of the entrepreneur is to introduce innovations in the economy and profits are a reward for this function. Schumpeter emphasized this function of the entrepreneur to distinguish him from the bureaucratic executive or the manager, who simply runs an established business in a steady manner. Invention may be made by a technician or an engineer, but when this technical invention is put to commercial use it becomes an innovation. An innovator is a businessman with vision and originality and dares to undertake high risks involved in a new business.

Innovations are of two types:

(i) **Product innovations:** those which reduce the cost of production of an entrepreneur. These include introduction of a new machinery, new and cheaper technique or process of production, exploitation of a new source of raw material, a new and better method of organising the firm etc. All these affect the cost and quality of the product.

(ii) **Market innovations:** those which increase the demand for his product. These include introduction of a new product, a new variety or design of the product, a new and superior method of advertisement, discovery of new markets etc. All these influence the market demand for the firm's products.

If an innovation proves successful i.e. if it achieves its aim of either reducing the cost of production or enhancing the demand for the product, it will give rise to profit. Profits emerge due to successful innovotion because either cost falls below the prevailing price of the product or the entrepreneur is able to sell more and at a better market price than before. This is described as **innovational profit.**

Profits caused by a particular innovation are only temporary and tend to be competed away as others imitate and also adopt them. When an entrepreneur introduces a new innovation, he is first in a monopoly position, for the new innovation is confined to him only. Therefore he makes large profits. When after sometime others also adopt it in order to get a share, profits will disappear.

But a successful innovator may search for another innovation and again he tends to earn innovational profit. In this way innovational profits appear and disappear. Therefore these innovational profits exist continuously in a modern progressive business.

Criticism:

Schumpeter's innovation theory can be criticized on the same grounds as Clark's dynamic theory.

(i) Schumpeter, also like Clark ignores uncertainty as a source of profit.

(ii) He also denies that risk-bearing plays any role in the determination of profits.

(iii) Critics point out that Schumpeter's theory explains nothing about windfall or monopoly profits. Such profits do not result from the introduction of innovations.

(iv) The theory has been considered unsatisfactory due to its explanation of profits as of temporary nature. Profits are neither temporary nor wiped out after a short time. Profits remain for a long time. In fact, if profits are wiped out soon, no entrepreneur will stick to the production process.

In short, innovation theory of profits is not a satisfactory and complete theory of profit. However, it points out a very important function of the entrepreneur which generates profits.

POINTS TO REMEMBER

1. **Distribution** means the sharing of the wealth that is produced among the different factors of production. There are two aspects of the distribution process.
   (i) Functional Distribution
   (ii) Personal Distribution
2. The Marginal Productivity Theory of Distribution also known as the General Theory of Distribution is a generalized theory of factor pricing for all factors of production.
3. Long-run equilibrium in the factor market is attained when ARP = AFC = MRP = MFC.
4. **Rent:** It is defined as the price paid for the use of land and other natural resources which are completely fixed in total supply. It is the unique supply conditions of land and other natural resources: their fixed supply: which makes rental payments distinguishable from wages, interest and profit payments.
5. **Ricardian Theory of rent:** According to Ricardo, rent is "that portion of the produce of the earth which is paid to the landlord for the use of the original and indestructible powers of the soil."
6. **Modern Theory of Rent**: The main propounder of the modern theory of rent is Mrs Joan Robinson. This theory is based on three important propositions:

(a) Rent arises due to scarcity of land.
(b) Rent is a generalised surplus earned by all factors.
(c) Rent, as a surplus, earned by a factor, is measured with reference to transfer earnings of the factor in its prevailing employment

7. **Quasi-Rent:** It refers to the short run earnings of some factors of production, which may be fixed in the short run but not in the long run. These factors of production include capital such as machines and other man-made instruments, factory buildings, ships etc.
8. **Wages:** The term 'wages' means, payments made for the services of labour. A wage payment is essentially a price paid for a particular commodity, namely labour services.
9. **Minimum Wages:** The minimum amount of remuneration that an employer is required to pay wage earners for the work performed during a given period, which cannot be reduced by collective agreement or an individual contract.
10. Money wages or nominal wages are the wages paid or received in terms of money per hour, per day, per week and so forth
11. Real wages are the quantity of goods and services which one can obtain with his money wages; real wages are the 'purchasing power' of money wages.
12. **Subsistence Wages:** They are wages that provide only the bare necessities of life.
13. **Fair wages:** These are minimum wage rates for specific occupations.
14. **Supply of labour:** The supply of labour means the number of hours of a given type of labour which will be offered for hire at different wage rates. Usually, the relationship between the price of labour (wages) and the total amount of labour supplied in the market is a direct one i.e. a greater quantity of labour is offered at rising wage levels.
15. **Backward bending supply curve of Labour:** Beyond a certain wage level, the workers preference for leisure becomes more dominant against their will to be work.
16. **Exploitation of Labour:** Labour is said to be exploited when the wage is less than the value of the marginal product (VMP), which is equal to the physical product multiplied by the sale price of the product. There are three types of exploitation –
    (i) Monopsonistic Exploitation
    (ii) Monopolistic Exploitation
    (iii) Double Exploitation

17. **Collective Bargaining:** The ongoing process of negotiation between representatives of workers and employers to establish the conditions of employment.
18. **Interest:** The price paid for the use of capital in any market.
19. **Profit:** Profit is the reward to the entrepreneur for his entrepreneurial functions. Among the four factors of production the entrepreneur occupies a unique place.

QUESTIONS FOR DISCUSSION

1. Explain the Marginal Productivity Theory of Distribution.
2. Explain the Ricardian Theory of Rent.
3. Explain the Modern Theory of Rent.
4. Distinguish between Economic Rent and Scarcity Rent.
5. Explain the concept of quasi-rent.
6. Distinguish between money wages and real wages.
7. Distinguish between Subsistence Wages and Fair Wages.
8. What are Minimum Wages?
9. What are the factors which influence supply of labour?
10. Explain the concept of work-leisure ratio.
11. When is the supply curve of labour backward bending?
12. What is collective bargaining? What are the circumstances under which collective bargaining may arise?
13. Explain the Modern theory of wages.
14. What is exploitation of labour? In which situations does exploitation of labour occur?
15. What role do trade unions play in wage determination?
16. Explain the Classical Theory of Interest.
17. Explain the Loanable Funds Theory of Interest.
18. Explain the Liquidity Preference Theory of Interest.
19. Distinguish between gross profits and net profits.
20. Explain the Dynamic Theory of Profits.
21. Explain the Risk and Uncertainty-bearing Theory of Profits.
22. Explain the Innovation Theory of Profits.

QUESTIONS FOR DISCUSSION

1. Define Rent. **[April 2009, Oct. 2009, April 2010]**
2. What is Collective Bargaining? **[April 2009, Oct. 2009, April 2010]**
3. What is Profit? **[April 2009, Oct. 2009, April 2010]**

   OR

   Define Profit. **[April 2010, Oct. 2010]**

4. What is Minimum Wages? [Oct. 2009]
5. What is Real Wages? [Oct. 2010]
6. What is Quasi Rent? [Oct. 2010]
7. Explain Concept of Quasi Rent. [April 2010]
8. Explain the Innovation Theory of Profit. [Oct. 2010]
9. State and Explain Ricardian' Theory of Rent. [April 2009, Oct. 2016]
10. Discuss 'Risk and Uncertainty Theory of Profit. [April 2010]
11. Explain Loanable Funds Theory of Interest. [April 2010]
12. Discuss Liquidity Preference Theory of Interest. [Oct. 2010]
13. Discuss Modern Theory of Rent. [April 2011]
14. Explain the Ricardian Theory of Rent. [April 2012]
15. Describe Liquidity Preference Theory of Interest. [April 2009]
    Explain Liquidity Preference Theory of Interest. [Oct. 2009]
    OR
16. Explain Marginal Productivity Theory of Distribution. **[Oct. 2009]**
    OR
    Critically examine Distribution Theory of Marginal Productivity. [April 2010]
17. Explain Ricardian Theory of Rent. [Oct. 2010]
18. Critically examine 'Loanable Funds Theory of Interest'. [April 2011]
19. Discus the Liquidity Preference Theory of Interest. [April 2012, 13]
20. State innovation Theory of Profit. [April 2013]
21. Explain Ricardian Theory of Rent. [April 2012]
22. State the Dynamic Theory of Profit. [Oct. 06, 07, April 2017]
23. Why the Supply Curve of Labour is Backward Sloping? [Oct. 06]
24. State and Explain Liquidity Preference Theory of Interest. [Oct. 07]
25. Explain the Modern Theory of Rent. [Oct. 06, 15, April 08, 16]
26. Critically examine Ricardian Theory of Rent. [April 2006]
27. Explain the Loanable Funds Theory of Interest. [Oct. 06, April 08]
28. Critically examine Marginal Productivity Theory of Distribution. [Oct. 07, April 08]
29. State and Explain Ricardian Theory of Rent. [April 09]

30. Describe Liquidity Preference Theory of Interest. [Oct. 09, 10, April 09]

31. Explain Marginal Productivity Theory of Distribution. [Oct. 09]

32. Explain Loanable Funds Theory of Interest. [April 10, Oct. 15]

OR

Critically Examine Loanable Funds Theory of Interest. [April 11]

33. Critically Examine Distribution Theory of Marginal Productivity. [April 10]

34. Explain Ricardian Theory of Rent. [Oct. 10, 16]

35. Discuss Modern Theory of Rent. [April 2011]

36. Discuss Liquidity Preference Theory of Interest. [April 12, 14, 15]

37. Write Short Notes : Background Sloping Supply Curve of Labour. [April 11, 12]

38. Discuss Risk and Uncertainty Theory of Profit. [April 10]

39. Explain concept of Quasi Rent. [April 10]

40. Explain the Innovation Theory of Profit. [Oct. 10]

41. State the Innovation Theory of Profit. [April 12]

42. Write Short Notes:

(A) Ricardian Theory of Rent [April 14, 18]

(B) Backward Sloping Supply Curve of Labour [April 14, Oct. 16]

(C) Innovation Theory of Profit. [April 14, 15, 17, 18]

(D) Modern Theory of Rent. [April 15]

(E) Quasi Rent. [Oct. 15]

(F) Dynamic Theory of Profit. [Oct. 15]

(G) Motives of Liquidity Preference. [April 16, 17, Oct. 17]

43. Explain the Backward Sloping Supply Curve. [April 15, 17]

OR

Explain the concept of Backward Sloping Supply Curve of Labour. [April 16]

44. Explain the Risk and Uncertainty Bearing Theory of Profit. [Oct. 17]

45. Discuss the Ricardian Theory of Rent. [Oct. 17]

■■■

Case Studies Approach

Case studies generate an in-depth, multifaceted understanding of an issue in the real life context. It is an empirical inquiry that investigates a phenomenon within its real life context. It explores the causes and implications of underlying principles. Case studies research quantitative evidence and are studied holistically.

Micro-economics is often perceived as being a theoretical subject with laws, theories and accompanying figures/diagrams with little significance in policy applications. Case study approach fosters analytical skills and enables the students of business economics a wide participation in economic disciplines. It enables the development of social skills and learning by doing.

1. **Using economic concepts explain the mushrooming of Malls and their growth**.

   The advent of malls since mid 2000 describes the manifestation of market power of large business corporate versus small competitors.

   - The case raises regulatory issues, from both the government perspective and supermarkets and consumers. The government has a vested interest in moving economic activity towards a generally more competitive context but at what cost might this be? Is it the government's responsibility to ensure the survival of 'Kirana' stores or do consumers also need to take some responsibility by supporting local stores in spite of the convenience offered by the big malls?
   - The basic principles of oligopolistic market structure; barriers to entry and interdependence price discrimination to understand the above case.
   - Economics of scale – competitive advantage consolidated through marketing advertising.
   - Favorable external factors such as growing consumer wealth and flexibility in job markets.
   - Growing barriers to entry as financial advantage secures wider access to property.

   The growth of malls (big chain stores) can partially be explained through the increased sophistication in marketing themselves and their products through visually impressive displays, the development of brands and direct advertising to consumers. Self service and economies of scale are also added advantages.

- The successful launch of loyalty cards enables a successful marketing campaign customized to customer's testes and preference.
- The product range is driven by consumer choice which is further differentiated by income, such that products are aimed at low income, middle income and the high end budget. For e.g. low income range is "value" or "economy" and the high end is "finest" or "taste the difference".
- The dominant malls are in a position to exercise significant power in their purchase of goods and services (Marketing or Commercial economics)

2. How is the success of a price fixing ring compromised by the growing number of participants?

- Oligopolistic market structure and associated interdependence identified.
- Collusion among the dominant firms through a price fixing agreement attempts to reduce uncertainly regarding the actions of others.
- The greater the numbers involved, the increased likelihood of detection and / or cheating by aggrieved members.
- **Baumol** suggests that the ideal number is 4 and 6 is too many.

Learning points from the concept of oligopolistic market structure:

- Industry dominance by a small number of large firms.
- Interdependence constraints on behavior
- Barriers to entry and abnormal profits
- Kinked demand curve.

3. Identify the oligopolistic features of the Car Market and suggest how the car market might differ if this had been a (perfectly) competitive environment

- Oligopolistic market features – few dominant retailers, nature of the branded product and significance of advertising.
- Competitive market structure – many buyers/ sellers, homogenous product, absence of barriers to entry.

Answers to the above question should incorporate diagrammatic illustrations.

4. **Perfect Competition in certain agriculture commodities such as food grains – Fact or Fiction?**
   - To understand the concept and operation of perfect competition in a real world.
   - Many important features of perfect competition like large number of buyers and sellers, information symmetry, low barriers to entry and to some extent homogenous products manifests in food grains business.
   - Given the assumptions of food grains market, whether it is a good example of a perfectly competitive market?
5. **Higher Education or a job as an Accountant - How much did that decision really cost you ?**
   - Concept of opportunity cost
   - Problem of scarcity explains why opportunity cost is the appropriate measure of cost.
   - Real cost of an action to society is the resources that are used when that action is taken.
   - Monetary price is an important part of opportunity cost. Time is also a resource and is also a part of opportunity cost.

   Deciding between a master's programme and a job as an accountant involves the following information relevant to calculating opportunity cost i.e.

   1. The fees of the programme
   2. Salary as an accountant in every future year of the working life
   3. Time spent in enhancing specialized skills and knowledge versus earning an income.
6. **Cost –Benefit Case Study – New Build Supermarket**
   - Cost-benefit analysis of the design stage of a project to construct a new supermarket with a certain value.
   - To calculate the total potential saving (Net of implementation cost).

   The case study will consist of calculating the potential costs and benefits of carrying out waste management good practice at the design stage of construction of the new supermarket. The method will identify the opportunities to reduce and recover waste and to estimate the cost savings from implementing these measures.
7. **Indian Stock Market and Perfect Competition**

   A stock exchange provides a market place, real or virtual, to facilitate the exchange of securities between buyers and sellers.

- Participants in the stock exchange range from small individual investors to large traders, who can be based anywhere in the world.
- By design a stock exchange resembles perfect competition.
- Large number of rational profit maximisers actively compare with each other.
- Important current information is almost freely available to all participants.
- Price of individual security is determined by market forces.

Learning points:

- In the short run, it is not easy for a market player to either exit or enter in those stocks which are under no delivery.
- In the long run players can exit the market if they are not able to earn profit and new investors are attracted by rise in market price.
- Though individual investors exit in very large numbers, average capital owned by a single large player is huge in comparison to small investors.
- Hence by design, an Indian Stock Market resembles perfect competition, not as a complete description but as an approximation.

8. Indian Railway and Price Discrimination:

- Indian Railways is the largest rail network in Asia.
- World's second largest under one management.
- Carries 13 million passengers everyday.
- Largest employer in the organized sector.
- Largest monopoly in the country charging different fares under various heads.

Learning points:

- Indian Railways charges different fares on the basis of consumer (passenger) categories such as normal fare, concessions for students, senior citizens etc.
- Different fares on the basis of class of travel - passengers travel the same distance by the same train, but pay differential fares for different levels of comfort.

- Different fares on the basis of category of train such as Rajdhani, Shatabdi, Superfast, Jan Shatabdi, Garib Rath, Mail/Express, Passenger and Shuttle - discrimination is on basis of time covered in travel.

9. Monopoly breeds Excess Capacity, Competition Expands horizons:

- Till about two decades ago, there was a wide gap between the number of telephones available and the demand for telephones. There were always about two million on the waiting list.
- When the Government opened the doors of investment to the private sector in 1994, it broke the monopoly of the Department of Telecommunications.

Learning Points:

- Prior to privatisation, monopoly in the telecom sector failed to utilize the excess capacity in this sector.
- After privatisation, investment funds flowed into this sector increasing the availability of telephone connections exponentially.
- This has bridged the gap between demand and supply considerably and there is no waiting period for phone connections.

10. David Fights Goliath - The Dwarf Fights the Giant - Nirma Fights Surf

- The 1960s and 1970s saw the selling of laundry detergents in the form of bars to most Indians and detergent powder was a luxury for the upper classes.
- Inception of a low cost detergent - Nirma in 1969.
- In a short span of time, Nirma created an entirely new market segment and emerged as a household brand.
- Hindustan Lever Limited (HLL) led the detergent powder market with its premier product - Surf.

Learning points:

- Nirma was able to keep the price of its detergent low by not using any high quality ingredients. Surf was affordable to an elite segment only due to its high price but Nirma became affordable to the common man.

- Nirma soon realized that it would have to launch products for the upper end of the market to retain its middle class consumers, who would graduate to the upper end. Hence in 1990 it ventured into the toilet soap market to target the premium segment.
- On the other hand, Nirma compelled HLL to change its strategies. The company decided to enter the low priced segment by positioning Wheel against Nirma.
- Nirma provides a classic example for a price-led marketing strategy that shattered the near monopoly of HLL.
- Nirma gave a new connotation to differentiation by creating a similar product available at much lower price.

11. Cartels - Violators of Competition:

- It is usually observed that there is simultaneous movement of interest rates by public sector banks.

Learning points:

- Simultaneous raising and cutting of interest rates could be due to cartelization.
- Banking is the largest sector which has come under the Competition Commission of India (CCI) lens.
- However, bankers refute the charge by the fact that interest rate movements are guided by RBI's monetary policy and liquidity conditions prevailing in the market.

12. Maruti Suzuki India as Market leader:

- Maruti Suzuki India's largest car manufacture announced price hike of around 2% to 3% of its complete product range in 2004.
- Again in 2008, it hiked the price of all its cars.
- During both the periods, the other car manufactures followed suit.

Learning points:

- Maruti Suzuki hiked its price in 2004 citing rise in cost of production.
- The other car manufacturers such as Mahindra and Mahindra, Tata Motors and Hyundai followed suit little later.
- Thus, whenever Maruti Suzuki - the market leader in car industry - hiked prices, others retaliated in a similar manner - a classic example of oligopolistic behaviour.

■■■

About the Author

Dr. (Mrs.) Girija Shankar, officiating Principal, Professor and **Head of Department Business Economics** at the **Ness Wadia College of Commerce, Pune** has been teaching Economics and Banking for three and half decades.

She has been a Member of the Board of Studies (Business Economics) for two tenures and also a Member of the Board of Studies (Banking and Finance) of Savitribai Phule Pune University (SPPU). She is a recognised Research Guide of SPPU for M.Phil and Ph.D in Economics and Banking. Several students have been awarded M.Phil and Ph.D and some are pursuing Ph.D under her guidance.

She has been empanelled as VC Nominee (SPPU) of Board of Studies in Economics at various autonomous institutions. She has been nominated as a Special Invitee Member at Faculty of Commerce and Management at RTM Nagpur University.

She has been the Course Co-ordinator, subject expert, developed curriculum and content writer for the development of E-content programmes in Economics and Banking and Insurance of MOOCs (Massive Open-Online Courte) launched on SWAYAM platform.

Dr. Girija Shankar holds an M.Phil. from the Gokhale Institute of Politcs and Economics, Pune and a Ph.D. in Business Economics from the University of Pune. She is a recipient of Teacher Fellowship for completion of Ph.D. under the UGC Faculty Improvement Programme. She has been a Resource Person and Evaluator at several Seminars, Workshops, Conferences, Faculty Development Programmers, Refresher Courses and refereed Research Projects. She has received awards for her contribution to teaching. She has traveled to Singapore, Germany and USA and studied the Pedagogy at Stanford University, USA; Purdue University USA; Nanyang Technological University, Singapore and Berlin Technical University, Germany.

She is a prolific writer and has authored several books and research papers.

■■■

www.ingramcontent.com/pod-product-compliance
Lightning Source LLC
LaVergne TN
LVHW082346171026
850499LV00040B/1344

SPPU New Syllabus

BUSINESS ECONOMICS

(Micro) - II

for

First Year B.Com. Semester - II

CBCS Pattern [Course Code 123]

As Per New Syllabus, June 2019

Dr. (Mrs.) Girija Shankar
Officiating Principal
Professor and Head of Department of Business Economics
Ness Wadia College of Commerce
Pune

NIRALI PRAKASHAN
ADVANCEMENT OF KNOWLEDGE

N5117

Business Economics (Micro - II) (F.Y.B.Com.) **ISBN 978-93-89686-52-4**

First Edition : December 2019

Published By:
NIRALI PRAKASHAN
Abhyudaya Pragati, 1312, Shivaji Nagar
Off J.M. Road, PUNE – 411005
Tel - (020) 25512336/37/39, Fax - (020) 25511379
Email: niralipune@pragationline.com

➢ **DISTRIBUTION CENTRES**

PUNE

Nirali Prakashan (For orders within Pune) : 119, Budhwar Peth, Jogeshwari Mandir Lane, Pune 411002, Maharashtra, Tel: (020) 2445 2044, Mobile: 9657703145 Email: niralilocal@pragationline.com

Nirali Prakashan (For orders outside Pune) : S. No. 28/27, Dhayari, Near Asian College Pune 411041 Tel: (020) 24690204; Mobile: 9657703143 Email: bookorder@pragationline.com

MUMBAI

Nirali Prakashan : 385, S.V.P. Road, Rasdhara Co-op. Hsg. Society Ltd., Girgaum, Mumbai 400004, Maharashtra; Mobile: 9320129587 Tel: (022) 2385 6339 / 2386 9976, Fax: (022) 2386 9976 Email: niralimumbai@pragationline.com

➢ **DISTRIBUTION BRANCHES**

JALGAON

Nirali Prakashan : 34, V. V. Golani Market, Navi Peth, Jalgaon 425001, Maharashtra, Tel: (0257) 222 0395, Mob: 94234 91860; Email: niralijalgaon@pragationline.com

KOLHAPUR

Nirali Prakashan : New Mahadvar Road, Kedar Plaza, 1st Floor Opp. IDBI Bank, Kolhapur 416 012, Maharashtra. Mob: 9850046155; Email: niralikolhapur@pragationline.com

NAGPUR

Nirali Prakashan : Above Maratha Mandir, Shop No. 3, First Floor, Rani Jhanshi Square, Sitabuldi, Nagpur 440012, Maharashtra Tel: (0712) 254 7129; Email: niralinagpur@pragationline.com

DELHI

Nirali Prakashan : 4593/15, Basement, Agarwal Lane, Ansari Road, Daryaganj Near Times of India Building, New Delhi 110002 Mob: 08505972553, Email: niralidelhi@pragationline.com

BENGALURU

Nirali Prakashan : Maitri Ground Floor, Jaya Apartments, No. 99, 6th Cross, 6th Main, Malleswaram, Bengaluru 560003, Karnataka; Mob: 9449043034 Email: niralibangalore@pragationline.com

Other Branches: Hyderabad, Chennai

niralipune@pragationline.com | www.pragationline.com

Also find us on www.facebook.com/niralibooks